# From Turnpike Gates to Christmas Waits

~

*Historical Notes from Village Life*

~

## Alan Dodge

*To Chins and Barbara,
with best wishes,
Alan Dodge
April 2012.*

EX LIBRIS PRESS

Published in 2012 by
Ex Libris Press
11 Regents Place
Bradford on Avon
Wiltshire   BA15 1ED
www.ex-librisbooks.co.uk

Origination by Ex Libris Press

Printed by CPI Group (UK) Ltd
Croydon, CR0 4YY

ISBN 978-1-906641-43-6

The ilustrations which appear in this book, including the cover, are
reproduced from Ackerman's edition of W.H. Pyne's *Microcosm*
which was first published in 1808

# CONTENTS

## 2008 ~

## 2009 ~

## 2010 ~

# FOREWORD

For seven years I wrote a brief historical note for the Parish Magazine of Freshford, Limpley Stoke and Hinton Charterhouse. These villages are on the Somerset/Wiltshire border around six or so miles south-east of Bath where the rivers Avon and Frome join. The notes were written in no planned sequence, but generally arose out of some observation or seasonal change. It so happened that the first in January 2004 was about turnpike gates and the last in December 2010 about the old carol singers – the Christmas waits, thus the title *From Turnpike Gates to Christmas Waits*. I have had a number of requests to collect them together, and this is the result!

*Alan Dodge*
*Freshford*
*2012*

*For our children, Christopher, Mary, Peter and Elizabeth:*
*a collection of things we often talked about.*

# 2004

# TURNPIKE GATES

The commencement of a new year is usually a time to think of the past as well as the future. It is appropriate that the name January is derived from Janus, the Roman god of doorways, passages and bridges, and who is usually depicted with two heads facing both ways. Looking both ways is a reminder of the numerous turnpike cottages that were built throughout England in the 18th and early 19th centuries, and from them traffic could be seen coming in both directions. The gate or turnpike would be opened if the appropriate fee was paid to travel on the toll-road. The travellers then proceeded on their journey.

The road through Hinton from Bath to Norton was turnpiked in 1752, and in 1787 was described as the way to Portsmouth, Southampton, Warminster and Salisbury. There was a gate on this road at Midford until 1879, although in 1853 'some evil-disposed persons did...wilfully and maliciously pull down and carry away the Turpike Gates.' A reward of £20 was offered by the Trustees of the Black Dog Roads for information on this crime. Other local gates were erected opposite the Hungerford Arms at Farleigh, opposite Tuckers Grave near Faulkland in 1768, and at the entrance to Crowe Lane in Freshford. These three toll cottages still remain. One erected by the Black Dog Trust at the Freshford end of Branch Road was demolished when this Trust was disbanded in 1879. When joining the A36 at this point today, one certainly has to look both ways!

*January 2004*

# VILLAGE NAMES

In the Domesday book of 1086, the villages of Hinton and Bathampton are both spelt HANTONE. This rather common name in England means a high or an important farmstead. It was an appropriate move at some time in past ages to add a distinguishing name to each as Charterhouse and Bath. There have been a number of small name changes in other local villages such as at Farleigh Hungerford which was known as Farleigh Montfort after the de Montfort family until the late 14th century.

Although we are so familiar with the names of the three villages in our parish, they all could have been quite different. Hinton was often referred to in the reversed manner as Charterhouse Hinton although in medieval times the appendage Monachorum seems to have had occasional use. Monachorum, meaning the place of monks is used today at Buckland Monachorum in Devon. The church of St Mary at Limpley Stoke appears to have formerly been dedicated to St Edith. Thus the village might have been called Stoke St Edith, or Stoke Edith as is a village in Herefordshire. In 1464 the parish of Freshford was joined to that of Woodwick. A joint ecclesiastical parish was formed and Woodwick church and village vanished, apart from field names. Thus our united Parish benefice might have been called Freshford cum Woodwick with Stoke St Edith and Hinton Monachorum!

*February 2004*

# A COTTAGE HOSPITAL

It is hard to imagine that there was a Cottage Hospital at Upper Mount Pleasant in Rosemary Lane, Freshford from 1897-1947. Called at its founding in the year of Victoria's Diamond Jubilee, the Queen Victoria Nursing Home, it was donated for the care of local villages from Norton St Philip to Winsley, by Mrs Mary Bythesea of Freshford Hall. Its work was largely supported by personal gifts, church and house to house collections, gifts of food and other goods, and a 'Linen League'. There was an Annual 'Egg Week' which in 1934 received 1,721 eggs for preserving. A resident nursing sister was supported by other nurses and assistants. In 1929 the accounts of the hospital included £1.10s.0d. for a bicycle. As the District Nurse could not ride a bicycle, 5 shillings were paid out for 'lessons in cycling for nurse'.

It was in great demand for maternity cases in the early years of the Second World War when the city was more vulnerable to air raids. When a patient was to be moved from an upper floor for an operation, the local farmer was often called in from the field nearby to lend a hand!

In former years villagers would have relied on herbal remedies and cures. Scabious, for example, still grows in the field called Nurlton behind the hospital. In 1597 *Gerard's Herbal* suggested that this plant 'scoureth the chest and lungs; it is good against an old cough, paine in the sides, and such like infirmities of the chest'.

*March 2004*

# LOCAL GOVERNMENT

On April 1st, 1974, exactly 30 years ago, Hinton Charterhouse, Freshford, and much of North Somerset, South Gloucestershire and Bristol were incorporated into the new County of Avon. Although the Shires of Somerset and Wiltshire were established in the middle of the ninth century, County Councils were not formed until about a thousand years later, in 1888. The end of this long historic link with Somerset was commemorated in Freshford by placing a 'memorial stone' on the Tyning on March 31st, 1974. As it happened, Avon County lasted only until 1997 when the Unitary Authority of Bath and North East Somerset was established. The link with the former Somerset County Council is still seen today in the letters SCC on the top of direction finger posts in Hinton and Freshford, although these letters are not picked out in black as in old Somerset.

There are still a few local reminders of Somerset on the roadside, for example on crossing the viaduct, leaving Limpley Stoke and entering Monkton Combe, a sign still shows Wiltshire and Somerset. A much older link with Somerset are the two FRESHFORD SLOW signs near The Inn, and in Church Lane with the initials SAC. This refers to Somerset Auto Club, which like the Wilts Auto Club, erected many cautionary and danger signs. These two are a remarkable survival from the 1920s or 30s, and their message is even more important 70 or 80 years later!

*April 2004*

# PEST CONTROL

Each of our villages has just completed the annual duty of electing churchwardens. This ancient office, possibly dating back to the tenth century, has been defined as 'the proper guardian and keeper of the parish church'. For hundreds of years the wardens kept the church accounts, and the oldest extant churchwardens' account book in England is from St Michael's Church Bath that dates from 1349. In our own parish, the accounts for St Mary's exist from 1747, St John's from 1760 and St Peter's from 1779. As responsible members of the local community the wardens were given other secular responsibilities.

One of these, from the reign of Henry VIII in 1532, was the village pest control officer. In practice, small sums of money were paid from the church rates for dead animals and birds that were thought to be vermin. Some examples from St Mary's: 1747, 7 foxes, one old fox ; 1755, Mr Fisher's boy for Hegogs; 1845, 40 young and 2 old sparrows, and in the same year 'no more sparrows to be paid out of church rates'.  At St John's in 1774 the wardens paid out almost £4 for 777 sparrows, in 1809 1 wizzel, and in 1823, for a viper. At St Peter's in 1779, 1 old fox with five cubs, a polecat and 350 sparrows. An otter in 1792, and 2 moles in 1809. The present day wardens are no doubt relieved to know that this aspect of their duty ceased in the middle of the 19th century.

*May 2004*

# TURNPIKES AND RAILWAYS

The A36, Warminster Road, originally called the Black Dog Road, was the last turnpike to be constructed in this area before the railway age. Rather like a modern motorway, it was built as a totally new road from Woolverton to Bath cutting across a whole series of roads and lanes. The road was surveyed by William McAdam, grandson of the famous road engineer J.L. McAdam, in the early 1830s and constructed between 1834-6. The eleven arch viaduct at Monkton Combe was completed in 10 months to the design of a Bath architect G.P. Manners. While McAdam surveyed on higher ground, a route for a railway from Bristol to London via the Limpley Stoke Valley was also being surveyed. This part of the line was not built however as Brunel took over this scheme in 1835, and decided to route the London line via Box and the Vale of the White Horse. This Great Western Railway line was opened in 1841. Railways were to have a serious effect on the turnpike system, and as has been written 'the construction traffic was to destroy their surfaces and the opening of the lines their revenue'.

A typical feature of all new turnpikes was hedging with hawthorn. One of the many alternative name for this plant is Quick, derived from the fact that this was a living (quick) fence, rather than one with inanimate post and wires. The use of this word is as in the Apostles' Creed 'the quick and the dead'.

*June 2004*

# WARNING BEACONS

The 60th anniversary of D-Day, the allied invasion of occupied Normandy, is being widely commemorated. Exactly 200 years ago England was itself on high alert for an invasion by Napoleonic forces. In May 1804 news came to Weymouth that the French were just off the coast or had landed. These villages in Somerset and Wiltshire were prepared for invasion from the south and a detailed census in 1803 had identified, among other things, men able to serve as volunteers and those who could act as a guerrilla force and stop the advance of the enemy by chopping down trees and digging up roads. As it happened the Napoleonic invasion did not materialise. If it had this area would probably been alerted by beacon signals initially conveyed from one of the eight signal stations on the Dorset coast, and then the firing of beacons inland. A message from the coast to Melbury Beacon (862 ft.) just south of Shaftesbury, would have been passed to Creech Hill (655 ft.) near Bruton, to Beacon Hill (944 ft.) north of Shepton Mallet on the Mendips, and from thence to Beacon Hill at Lansdown. In the immediate locality a signal would probably have been conveyed by church bells. The beacons were manned by keepers who lived in makeshift huts, generally made of turves but with a brick chimney. According to Thomas Hardy's description in *The Dynasts*, there was a rick of furse for a quick fire, and another of wood for a longer slow burn for up to two hours.

*July 2004*

# SCOUTING

A facsimile edition of Robert Baden-Powell's influential book of 1908, *Scouting for Boys*, has recently been published. The writing of this book followed Baden-Powell's first experimental scout camp on Brownsea Island in 1907. Boy Scout groups were soon formed in towns and villages across the country, and one of the first Somerset Scout Camps was held in the meadowland around the confluence of the Avon and Frome rivers at Freshford between August 1st and 10th 1912. Altogether there were 12 separate camps in the valley for troops from places such as Cheddar and Wincanton, and with a headquarters camp on the higher ground near Freshford Manor. Each camp had a signal station which could be seen from the headquarters flagstaff. Among the activities of the camp was bridge building across the River Frome, and the erection of a breeches buoy across the River Avon after the firing of a rocket.

The Bishop of Bath and Wells, the elderly Right Revd. George Kennion, visited the camp and preached at the Sunday service. He was persuaded to cross the river in the breeches buoy, but was more fortunate than later passengers who, due to technical problems, were given an unceremonial baptism in the river! Some scouts cycled as far as Warminster, and by using a primitive mobile phone, a morse code transmitter, were able to report their arrival. Other activities included sports and ambulance work, and a prearranged attack by Wiltshire scouts from Castle Combe. The camp ended with a firework display and a torchlight tattoo.

*August 2004*

# POST BOXES

The oldest letter box still in use in England is at Barnes Cross at Pulham in Dorset which dates from the early 1850s. There are still a number of fine Penfold-type (named after the designer) Victorian boxes in Bath, such as at Laura Place. These are hexagonal with an acanthus leaf decoration on the top. In our three parishes we have boxes remaining from the reign of Victoria to our present queen, apart from the short reign of Edward VIII. In the wall of the Old Post Office at Hinton Charterhouse is the now unused letter box with Queen Victoria's cipher VR, and the wording POST OFFICE - LETTER BOX. Some years ago this was stolen, but fortunately it was retrieved from a Bath antiques market! A similar box is shown on a late 19th century photograph of Morris's Stores, Freshford, when this was also the Post Office. This would appear to have been recently replaced by a vertical box in the wall. (The earliest letter boxes all had vertical apertures). A wall-mounted box from the reign of Edward VII is still in use at Park Corner where it was installed in 1907. The wall-mounted boxes at Limpley Stoke and Freshford Post Offices both have the cipher GR but at Freshford has the additional VI. This indicates that it was installed in the reign of George VI, (1936-1952). The GR alone is an indication of the reign of George V (1910-1936). The remaining boxes within these parishes are all from the present reign and include wall-mounted ones at Middle Stoke and Sharpstone, and so-called lamp letter boxes at Midford Lane, Pipehouse, and Hinton Post Office.

*September/October 2004*

# YEW TREES

A feature common to our three churchyards, as to almost all churchyards in England, is the possession of yew trees. The common yew, *Taxus baccata*, is one of only three native British conifers, the others being Scots Pine and Juniper. The name yew might be derived from *iw*, an ancient word meaning green. Because of their great longevity, linked to ideas of immortality, they were planted in prehistoric times at burial sites. Often these sites were taken over as places of Christian worship and churches built. There are many yews in England that appear to predate their church, such as that at Tisbury in Wiltshire which is thought to be between 3,000 and 4,000 years old. The tree to the right of the church path at Freshford, according to calculations of its girth, is a youngster of around 1,000 years old; however this is at least 450 years older than the oldest part of St Peter's church.

In Medieval times yew foliage was used to decorate churches on Palm Sunday. Edward I in 1307 decreed that yews should be planted near church doors for shelter and also to protect the building from winds and storms. They could also be used in emergency for weapons, although most English longbows were made from wood from Spain and Italy. This feature of warfare together with the very poisonous nature of the foliage gave rise to Shakespeare's epithet in Richard II of the 'double fatal yew.' Indirectly the poisonous nature of the tree made farmers and land owners of the adjacent fields keep the churchyard walls in good order, otherwise their animals might be poisoned.

*November 2004*

# HOLLY

Holly, probably more than any other plant, is inextricably associated with Christmas. The association with festivities appears to go back to Greek and Roman times, and its symbolic characteristics of thorns, berries like blood, and white flowers like snow, were easily subsumed into medieval celebration. It is not surprising that this symbolism was incorporated into carols such as *The Holly and the Ivy*. Holly was therefore encouraged for church decoration at Christmas. In our own local Churchwardens' Account Books are occasional references to the purchase of holly, such as for St Mary's in 1829 'For holly to ornament the church', and for St Peter's in 1870 'Holly for church at Christmas, two shillings'. As with domestic decoration in those times, this was done on Christmas Eve. Large boughs of holly were often hoisted on to church walls and pew fronts, and in some places holes were drilled into the old box pews to take holly sprigs.

There are still many holly bushes in our local hedges and woods, a reminder of the days when the wood was also used for threshing flails, and the bushes themselves along with boundary stones were used as boundary markers. When the country was mapped in detail by the Ordnance Survey in the 19th century, the large scale maps noted 'B.S.' (boundary stone), 'stump' and sometimes 'Holly Bush', an indication of how our forefathers knew the extent of their parish boundaries and thus their parochial responsibilities.

*December 2004*

# 2005

# MILESTONES

Turnpike roads were a major feature of our transport system between 1663 and 1883. Travel was possible on these roads provided that a toll was paid. From 1766 all Turnpike Trusts were obliged to mark every mile with a marker 'denoting the distance of every such stone or post from London or any other place as shall seem meet.' Stage coach travel was increasing, and this enabled drivers to keep to schedules and timetables. In spite of the passage of time and the removal of most milestones during the Second World War a number still remain in our locality. The earliest stones were actually of stone with incised letters. These were followed by those which were stone with a cast-iron plate, and finally those of cast-iron alone.

On both Brassknocker and Widcombe Hills are fine cast-iron examples inscribed with 'Bath Turnpike Trust'. There are a number of very typical flat classical looking cast-iron ones of the Black Dog Trust at Midford, Norton St Philip and Woolverton. The one at Midford states 'Bath 4, Warminster 13, Frome 9.' Near the church at Norton St Philip is a good example of the Buckland (Dinham) Trust declaring 'London 104 miles'. One which has been overlooked because its iron plate has been removed is in the wall of Temple Court on The Hill in Freshford. This road was initially turpiked by the Tinhead Trust as part of a route from Bath to Salisbury in the 1750s. This Trust was taken over by the Trowbridge Trust in 1768.

*January 2005*

# FIELD NAMES

A most familiar feature of our local countryside is the arrangement of the land into fields enclosed by hedges, walls or fences. In olden times the word 'field' generally referred to the large, open, arable fields that were part of medieval and later farming, while enclosed areas were called closes, or tynings (tinings). Large open fields were often identified geographically before enclosure as in Hinton in the 17th century as South Field or North Field. A study of local field names from old deeds and maps reveals that the 150 or so names within our three parishes, many of which were used two to three hundred years ago with some slight etymological shifts.

There are a number called Tyning, and the most familiar of these is in Freshford between the village centre and Sharpstone, and was called Home Tyning in the late 18th century when it was a field of Freshford Farm, located at the church end of the High Street. One in Limpley Stoke off Midford Lane was called Wall Tining indicating the method of enclosure. Other features which figure prominently are names of size such as Sixteen Acres, or The Big Field; names of crops grown, such as Hop Garden or Turnip Close; names associated with the condition of the land or when it was used, such as Poor ground and Summerleaze; and the names of former owners such as Russell's Upper Ground, Willis's Leaze, and one near Brett Farm in Limpley Stoke delightfully called Mogg's Apple Tree.

*February 2005*

# STORMY WEATHER

Although weather is a major subject of our conversation, it is soon forgotten apart from particularly spectacular events such as the winters of 1947 and 1963, and the hurricanes in 1987 and 1990. People living in the West Country in the early 19th century would have remembered the 'Great Gale', as it was called, of November 23rd, 1824. On the Dorset coast 100 lives were lost, and the village of Fleet and its church were almost totally destroyed. Damage was widespread across Western England and the lead roof of St Mary's Church, Limpley Stoke, was blown off. According to the churchwardens' accounts of the time, repair was soon put in hand. 'Thomas Williams one day assisting the plumber when the lead was blown off the chapel. Mr Henry France for coal to make fire to melt the solder. Mr Allen for stone when the lead was blown off the chapel.'

A few years earlier, in 1814, the tower of this church had undergone a major repair and the expenses for this task are quite revealing of how the work was accomplished. 'Hauling three fir trees to make scaffold, including Turnpikes. Two wagon loads of stone and hauling from Combe Down and turnpikes. For hauling 108 gallons water to Stoke Church and turnpikes.' Major work was needed on this tower in more recent times after a lightning strike in July 1952. On this occasion the whole spire had to be rebuilt.

*March 2005*

# PARISH BOUNDARIES

Parish boundaries are not so important today as they were in former times. Until major local government changes in the 19th century, each parish was not only a separate ecclesiastical unit, but was also responsible for all social services, through the overseers of the poor; for the non-turnpiked roads the waywardens; and for good behaviour through the parish constables.

In a tradition going back hundreds of years, village boundaries were perambulated yearly well into the 19th century to show, in an era before good maps, the extent of the parish's responsibilities. People who were unfamiliar with the boundaries were encouraged to join in the boundary walk, and children were beaten on boundary tree stumps or stones to 'take pains' to remember where the boundary was. This was usually done on Ascension Day as the Freshford Vestry Minutes of 1839 stated: 'a perambulation of the boundaries of this parish to take place on Holy Thursday, according to ancient custom.' In 1779 the Freshford churchwardens paid for cakes and beer for the sustenance of the boundary walkers, and for the hire of a boat for the river sections. The total distance travelled would have been about seven miles. In the much larger parish of Hinton Charterhouse the boundary distance would have been over ten miles, while Limpley Stoke, being part of the vast parish of Bradford extending to Holt and Atworth, the distance would have been nearer 30 miles.

*April 2005*

# LOST VILLAGES

It is hard to believe that in England between the years 1300 an 1500, over three thousand villages vanished. Of this vast number two were from this immediate area. Within the west end of the present parish of Freshford was another village with its own parish church known at the time of the Domesday Book in 1086 as *Undewiche*, and later *Woodwick*. Economically it was not possible to support two churches and two priests, and Woodwick church closed in 1464. Many fields around Peipards Farm are still called Woodweeks, but the exact site of the church and its dedication are unknown.

The other local lost village was situated on the lane between Farleigh Hungerford and Westwood. In 1086 this was called *Wittenham*, but later *Rowley*. This had a church dedicated to St Nicholas, but it fell into disrepair after the villages of Farleigh and Rowley were amalgamated around 1428. Walter, Lord Hungerford, then built a new church of St Leonard (the present church) in the village, leaving the old one as his private chapel in the castle, and Rowley was abandoned. As with Woodwick, the community gradually drifted away, leaving only a series of earthworks in fields. The income which had supported Rowley church had been diverted to build and support the new church of St Leonard. Although there had been an obligation to maintain the church of St Nicholas and to hold three services each year, this did not appear to happen.

*May 2005*

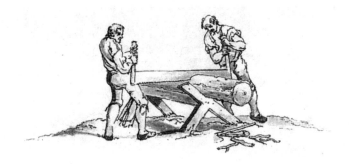

# PEST CONTROL

The screech of barn owls at night recently reminded me of the importance of owls in former times to the farmer in keeping down pests. Until the coming of the combine harvester and durable bins for grain storage, unthreshed sheaves were stored for some considerable time, and a farmer's awareness of and co-operation with the natural world was especially important. Many threshing and storage barns, such as the one at Hillside Farm in Freshford, were built with owl holes to encourage these birds to roost and thus keep down vermin that ate the stored grain. According to Gilbert White, writing in 1767, young barn owls needed a constant supply of fresh mice, whereas the young brown owl was less discriminating. Incidentally, White also established that all owls hoot in the key of E flat!

Granaries and ricks were often built on staddle stones, stone-like mushrooms, that are still found in gardens and roadsides as ornamental decorations. They, like the monkey-puzzle tree to the monkey, were supposed to be impossible to climb by mice and rats. Rats became an increasing problem in the 18th century with the arrival in Britain of the more troublesome brown rat which has almost totally displaced the black rat that had been here since the 12th century.

Sometimes granaries were built at first-floor level and with an outside staircase. Those were the days when most dogs and cats were working animals and not pets. Farm dog kennels were usually put under the stairs of these granaries so the dogs were on hand to catch marauding rats, and the granary door often had a small cat hole for feline control of mice.

*June 2005*

# NATURAL POWER

The use of wind and water in power generation is now very topical, but it is only a return to a time before the coming of the steam and internal combustion engines. In this area there were water-driven corn grinding mills from Norman times, and some, such as the one on the Wellow Brook at Midford, worked well into the 20th century. Others in this parish at Iford and Freshford on the river Frome, and at Limpley Stoke on the River Avon, became fulling mills. In the case of Freshford and Limpley Stoke Mills, they became substantial cloth manufactories. Dunkirk Mill was built in 1795 as a new yarn spinning mill on the stream from Pond Farm, but because of the limited water flow needed a 32 foot diameter waterwheel to drive the machinery. This mill was derelict for many years until restoration in the 1970s when a water-driven electricity generator was installed for domestic use. A remarkable restoration is currently taking place at Tellisford Mill, where in the former fulling mill a large water-driven generator is being installed. When functional this could supply electricity to at least 40 homes. The potential of the 16 old mill sites between Freshford and Frome on the River Frome is thus considerable!

Water was not only a source of power, but a vital factor in the placing of settlements in the days before piped water. The old cottages clustering around the pump at Park Corner, Freshford, illustrate this. For the high village of Hinton Charterhouse water supply was often a problem, but solved by the use of the natural power of a wind pump. This one was erected near Hinton Barn on the Norton Road in 1895, and gave the village a wind-driven water supply until 1923. The pump was made by the still existing engineering firm of John Wallis Titt of Warminster, who were well known throughout England for their 'wind engines'.

*July 2005*

# ROAD ACCIDENTS

Unfortunately road accidents occur from time to time, although every effort is now made to reduce their incidence by the use of speed restrictions, calming measures, white lines and so on. In the days of horse-drawn road travel, accidents were quite common, often due to the bad state of roads. An accident happened to Parson Woodforde (the famous diarist) as he was leaving Frome for Bath in a chaise in October 1793. On a narrow hill, this small vehicle was met by a large waggon pulled by eight horses, the chaise was overturned and badly damaged but no one was injured.

Another clergyman diarist, John Skinner of Camerton, also had a number of accidents, due sometimes to inadequate braking on steep hills, or in one case in the ice where his horses could not stand, and slid down on their haunches! While travelling near Axbridge on horseback in 1830, he was knocked to the ground by a horse and carriage. As he wrote in his journal 'his first feeling was that of anger against the awkward fellow who had occasioned my degradation, but lo and behold! I found it was the Bishop of Bath and Wells'.

Today we are able to identify vehicles by their number plates, but in those days every vehicle was obliged by law to have the name of the owner and the place of their abode painted in large legible letters for 'the better discovery of offenders'. The law was enforced by local magistrates, such as Thomas Horner of Mells who recorded in his notebook for 1770, 'Jacob Grove convicted of using his cart on the turnpike road at Frome without having his name painted thereon. Fine £5.'

*August 2005*

# TRAFALGAR

October 21st marks the 200th anniversary of the Battle of Trafalgar. This sea battle, arguably the most famous encounter in British naval history, was fought off Cape Trafalgar, just south of Cadiz in Spain. If such an event had taken place today, we would have heard of it in a matter of seconds in up to date news flashes and bulletins. Not so two hundred years ago! We do not know how long it took for news of this encounter to reach our villages. No doubt it was faster to here than to some remote parts of the country because of the proximity to Bath and Bristol.

The rector of Over Stowey, William Holland, kept a diary of these times, and news of this battle took over two weeks to reach his part of west Somerset. He wrote on November 6th, 'My wife went out to Mrs Woodhouse's and returned with the important news of Lord Nelson's victory over the combined fleets of France and Spain off Cadiz. But what has struck a damp on the whole is the death of the gallant Nelson'. On November 9th he saw a newspaper which gave details of the encounter, and how 'Nelson decoyed the enemy out of port and then fell upon them with a much larger fleet than they expected.'

While this momentous event was taking place, the quiet life of rural Somerset carried on. In this day's diary entry Rev'd Holland expresses his frustration with the gardening of his servant John, and then makes a delightful sweeping comment, 'the Somersetshire people are certainly slow and unenergetic, very large and strong but lazy and motionless, very ignorant yet very conceited.'

*September/October 2005*

# POUNDS

A feature of pre-enclosure open field agriculture was the possession of a village or manor pound or pinfold for confining stray animals. Cattle, sheep and pigs were a problem when they found their way into arable crops. Medieval manorial court records have numerous references to such problems with fines or punishment for the offending owners. In course of time most manors/villages had a small walled enclosure constructed somewhere near the centre of the community. A fine was paid to have one's animals released, although there are many records of illegal pound breaking.

We are fortunate that the pounds exist in Hinton Charterhouse and Freshford. At Hinton near the main entrance to the churchyard are the remains of a small walled enclosure, while at Freshford there is an easily overlooked walled enclosure on the village centre side of the cemetery in Freshford Lane. These two pounds have survived, no doubt, because they were constructed of stone. In many parts of south-east England they were constructed of timber with posts and rails, and in almost all cases have decayed away. In medieval times the manorial officer responsible for the pound was called the pinder, and he joins a number of other manor officials such as hayward, reeve and beadle whose name are perpetuated, but whose function has long gone.

*November 2005*

# THE POLICE

The establishment of County Police after an Act of Parliament in 1839, took away from each village the responsibility of appointing its own parish constables, an office which can be traced back to around 1242. Whereas the County of Wiltshire was one of the first to establish a county force, Somerset delayed until 1856. Freshford in 1844 appointed eight constables who lived in different parts of the village, and who acted as an early form of neighbourhood watch. One included Silas Miles, a blacksmith, who lived in the village centre. Blacksmiths were often sought after for this task because of their strength when the manhandling of offenders was needed, as well as their ability to make handcuffs or other restraining irons.

A village constable was called out in Hinton Charterhouse in 1836 after a drunken disturbance following a Friendly Society meeting in a public house. It was reported that 'in vain did he attempt to bring them to order, and to send them home; they took his staff and broke it; derided him for being a King's servant; threw him down and held him on the ground.'

In 1888 there was a violent disturbance at Limpley Stoke Manor House. This was beyond the control of the local constable, and 24 policemen from the Wiltshire County force quickly arrived by train at Limpley Stoke station from Bradford and Trowbridge, and were able to restore order!

*December 2005*

# 2006

# WOODLAND

Woodland is a familiar and often unnoticed part of our background scenery. Before the availability of coal, then gas, electricity and oil, wood was essential for almost all domestic energy needs. A glance at the Domesday Book of 1086 shows that there was extensive woodland in Hinton, in total one league long and half a league wide. This is an area approximately three miles by a mile and a half, and would probably embrace what we know as Friary Wood, Hog Wood, Cleaves Wood etc. For the Anglo-Saxon or Norman cottager, there were certain rights allowed by the lord of the manor: the right to fuel that could be reached 'by hook or by crook;' the so-called house-bote, the right to take wood for the repair of his cottage, and the right of pannage, which enabled the cottager to release his pigs into the wood to eat acorns and beech mast at certain times of the year. The name Hog Wood near the Priory may be derived from this custom.

In a survey of the Manor of Hinton in 1638 most of the woods were regarded as being coppice, cut down every ten or so years to give a crop of fuel, posts and faggots for bread ovens and so on. A distinction was made of Hog (Hogges) Wood in which oak trees in particular would be grown on to give timber for beams, carts and ploughs as well as producing coppice-like underwood.

*January 2006*

# FORDS AND BRIDGES

The frequency of the suffix 'ford' in numerous local place and hamlet names, is an indication on the importance of river crossings before bridges were constructed. For example, between Freshford and Frome on the River Frome are Iford, Stowford, Tellisford, Shawford, and Old Ford. Nearby on the River Avon are Bradford and Bathford, and on the Wellow Brook, Midford and the small farm called Ford between Hinton and Wellow. In addition there was a ford on the Avon at Limpley Stoke that was bridged by Stokeford Bridge in about 1740 and another called Blackwell Ford at Freshford Mill at the bottom of Rosemary Lane, bridged around 1800.

Many fords were bridged from the 12th century onwards with money provided by individuals, or with the encouragement of local monastic houses. One of the earliest local bridges still standing is at Iford which was built around 1400, although the statue of Britannia was erected only about a hundred years ago. Money was left for the rebuilding of Freshford Bridge in 1530, and this suggests that the original bridge was from the same period as Iford Bridge. The present Freshford Bridge was built in 1782.

Although 'bridge' is also part of English place names, it crops up rarely in this locality, apart from Trowbridge. This settlement is on the small River Biss, which could have easily be bridged by tree trunks, thus the origin of the name from Old English *treow brycy* = tree bridge. It is interesting that the Old English word ford is still used in the Welsh language as *ffordd* to indicate a way.

*February 2006*

# RAILWAYS

The long awaited raising of the up platform at Freshford Station has been in progress at night time over the last few months. This will make access to, and exit from trains coming from Bath safer and easier. When opened in February 1857 this was a single-track Broad Gauge line as used by the Great Western Railway. In 1875 the Broad Gauge was phased out to be replaced by the national Standard Gauge of four feet, eight and a half inches. The task of reducing the width of 110miles of line in this area took only five days! Ten years later in 1885 another major change occurred with the doubling of the line from Bradford to Bathampton. This was also a large undertaking with a new brickbuilt, 114 yard long viaduct across the River Avon at the confluence with the River Frome.

Now on an average weekday thirty or so trains will stop at Freshford Station. This is far cry from the bleak year of 1966 that brought disaster to our local railways. The Beeching Report had recommended the closure of Freshford, Limpley Stoke and Avoncliff stations, as well as the complete closure of the Somerset and Dorset line through Midford from Bath to Bournemouth. Freshford and Avoncliff were reprieved, but on March 6th 1966 Midford station closed together with the whole of the S. and D. line. On October 3rd Limpley Stoke Station closed.

Now 40 years on, part of the track-bed at Midford towards Wellow forms part of the Colliers Way cycle track between the Dundas Aqueduct, Radstock and Frome. Meanwhile an active campaign is underway to open the mile long Combe Down tunnel and to restore this for cyclists and walkers.

*March 2006*

# A VILLAGE WHEELWRIGHT

The discovery of a wheelwright's tyring platform during building work opposite the surgery in Freshford is an interesting reminder of the work of this important village craftsman before the days of motor transport. The Marchant family had been blacksmiths in the village for much of the 19th century, and had built a new forge on the site in 1877. Richard Marchant was first described in a Somerset Directory of 1889 as 'wheelwright' and his name appears as such until 1927. In 1935 his photograph appeared in a *National Daily* under the title of 'How to be Happy at 88'. Even at this age he was still able to make a wooden cart wheel. This family business evolved, like so many others, and it became 'Male and Marchant, Builders and Decorators.' They continued in business until around 1980.

The tyring platform is a metal disc about five feet in diameter. A completed wooden wheel was securely attached to this and then a red hot metal tyre was placed on it. After this had been hammered on, the tyre was cooled with water and it thus shrunk onto the wheel.

The sights and sounds in the village would have been so different in these times. From the wheelwright's there would have been loud hammering, together with smoke and steam. Further along the lane there would have been a strong smell of brewing, with its attendant plumes of steam, from the brewery attached to the Greyhound Inn and even more from the large brewery and maltings of Richard Forster. At the top of Church Hill a delightful smell of baking would have emanated from Morris's Bakery. Beer and bread would be delivered to villages around by cart and wagon, with wheels probably made and maintained by Richard Marchant.

*April 2006*

# OLD HOUSES

It is fascinating to think that some of the houses and cottage sites in our villages might have been in almost continuous occupation since before Norman times – over a thousand years. The Domesday Book of 1086, although not mentioning dwellings as such, did so by implication, as it refers to a number villagers and smallholders. These families would have lived in small wooden dwellings, which later on would have been constructed of stone. The question is thus often asked, how old is my house? In fact some parts of the foundation stonework or reused wooden beams might go back to these medieval times.

In our locality it is a surprise to know that in Lower Westwood house number 86 has a Norman undercroft dating from around 1200, two hundred or so years before the oldest portion of Westwood Manor. Wick Farm near the Brown Shutters crossroads on the A36 at Farleigh Hungerford has roof timbers that have been examined by tree ring dating to be from 1327, thirty or forty years older than Farleigh Castle. Parts of The Hermitage at Sharpstone, Freshford, including a staircase and roof timbers, appear to date from the 1400s, roughly contemporary with the tower of St Peter's Church.

We are able to date the year of building of some more recent houses, as they have a date stone on the façade, often with the initials of the owner or builder. There are a number of examples in our villages with dates from the early 18th century to the present day.

*May 2006*

# BARNS

As the weather becomes warmer, cereal crops planted in the autumn are beginning to grow more rapidly. In the days before the use of the reaper and binder, threshing machine and combine harvester, the tasks of harvesting and threshing involved an immense amount of manual work. On some farms threshing took place from October to May, and as the Wiltshire poet Stephen Duck wrote from his own experience week after week, we this dull task pursue. Around our villages there are a few barns that would have been used for manual threshing. Most have been converted into residences or other farm uses, but some, such as the fine stone-tiled barn at Peipards Farm at Freshford, are almost unchanged from the hand threshing times of two hundred years ago. The most common feature of these barns is the presence of two large doors on each side allowing loaded wagons to enter for unloading after waiting on the threshold. Threshing usually took place in the centre between these doors, allowing air movement, so there was less dust for the threshers, and also for blowing away the chaff when the grain was winnowed.

The word barn is derived from an Old English word *beren*, meaning barley room, thus the place name Berwick is derived from *bere-wic*, or barley farm. Locally, the most magnificent barn is at Barton Farm in Bradford on Avon, built around six hundred years ago on this erstwhile grange farm of Shaftesbury Abbey.

*June 2006*

# TIME

On a recent visit to west Cornwall, we were told that an old sun dial on the south porch of a church gave a time of 20 minutes later than London time. This was Cornish local time until the first half of the 19th century. With the coming of the railways, time throughout England was standardised and was often referred to as Railway Time. At that time the idea of 'being on time' was coined, and there was a considerable demand for the production and sale of pocket watches.

In medieval times there would have been little awareness of exact time. Workers in the fields would have heard bells ringing for church services during the day, and the time of these was often indicated to the priest by mass or scratch dials. (These were like small sundials scratched on the wall.) There is one on the south porch of All Saints church Tellisford.

During the 17th and 18th centuries, clocks became more common in church towers, but were initially without dials, the hours being indicated by a striking bell. Freshford's old tower clock was replaced by a new striking one by William Hallett of Bradford in 1860. Unusually for church clocks, his name is prominently displayed on the new dial. This could have been good advertising for Mr Hallett, a watchmaker, jeweller and ironmonger of Market Street Bradford. A few years before he had failed to get the contract for the restoration and maintenance of the tower clock in Holy Trinity Church, Bradford, so was perhaps keen to show what he could do. 146 years later, with the occasional drop of oil and adjustment, his clock still keeps excellent Railway Time!

*July 2006*

# HOPS

The naming of inns and public houses with conspicuous signs was a legal requirement from the 14th century. The George (named after St George) at Norton St Philip is thought to have been an inn for about six hundred years, although the name The George has not been found earlier than 1595. The Hop Pole at Limpley Stoke has a most attractive sign showing hops growing on a bine. The hop (the cone-like female flower) is still grown commercially in parts of Kent and Worcestershire, but is not now normally associated with this area. Hops have been used since the 16th century to give the typical bitter flavour to beer.

Although it might seem strange to have The Hop Pole as a local inn name, it appears that before the 19th century hops were grown over a much wider area of England when farmers and landowners grew their own hops and brewed their own beer. There is a well preserved brew house at Lacock Abbey, for example. A map of Hinton Abbey Farm, then centred on the former Carthusian Priory buildings and drawn in 1785, shows a field between the farm buildings and Hog Wood called Hop Garden.

A recently published work on farming in 17th century Wiltshire shows that a number of farmers in the Salisbury area and some as far north as Bromham had small hop gardens. Around our local hedgerows one can often find hop bines climbing over other vegetation for support, and producing a good harvest of hops. Some of these are probably an escape from our forefathers' hop gardens.

*August 2006*

# OLD ROADS

One can still appreciate what travel was like in England in olden times by walking between Pipehouse and Midford. This old trackway is so rough and isolated that one can easily imagine passing a medieval pilgrim or packhorse. Travel in the 13th century was such a hazardous business that a statute was passed that 'highways be widened where there are woods, or hedges, or ditches, so there be no place where a man may lurk to do evil near the road, for two hundred feet on either side.' This did not include the felling of oaks or 'great trees'.

In the 18th century there was another law to restrict the growth of such trees by roads 'because their droppings after rain injure the road, and their shade prevents it from drying'. In olden times roads were not so constricted by hedges, walls or fences, and they meandered around a waterlogged patch, a fallen tree or any other obstruction. In time these meanders became more permanent, and give the charm that we find today.

Something of the feeling of old roads is obtained by taking any of the three lanes from the Green area of Hinton Charterhouse towards the Warminster Road. The middle lane leading to Iford still has very wide verges. In medieval times these verges were often settled by squatters whose settlement became permanent as a long narrow garden plot. Such gardens are found throughout England and locally in lower Pipehouse Lane, and on the Faulkland Road at Norton St Philip. In Manorial times such encroachment was known as purpresture.

*September/October 2006*

40

# PIGS AND PANNAGE

Recently a number of pigs have been released into the New Forest to forage for acorns. There has been such an excellent crop from oak trees this year that grazing horses and ponies might be poisoned if they eat too many. In medieval times, peasants were allowed to release their pigs into the lord's woodland to forage for acorns, beech mast and others fruits as an ancient right, provided that the appropriate rent, known as pannage, was paid. Foraging was normally allowed between 29th August and 31st December. After this point the pigs were usually killed and salted down.

In the time of Domesday Book (1086) the Manor of Hinton was well wooded and included on the estate 90 pigs. This was an exceedingly high number for a Somerset manor. Other local manors had more typical numbers: Norton 28, Freshford 15, and Farleigh (Hungerford) 3. Today there is still extensive woodland with oak trees in the parish including Friary Wood, Cleaves Wood and the appropriately named Hog Wood. Since Domesday, the parish has been called successively Hinton Earls (after the Earls of Salisbury who owned the manor), Hinton Monachorum (the place of monks from the presence of the Priory after 1232) and finally Hinton Charterhouse. In Dorset a small village on the river Toller near Maiden Newton also had many pigs on its manorial estate and was called in medieval times the place of pigs i.e. Toller Porcorum. Hinton Porcorum would have made a very distinctive village name!

*November 2006*

# WATER SUPPLY

Although piped water came to most dwellings in our villages during the first half of the 20th century, a number of houses are still reliant on spring water alone. These include cottages at Friary, Woodside Cottages at Staples Hill, and Brett Farm in Limpley Stoke. Prior to the coming of mains water, most cottages and houses had been located near to a spring, pump or well. At Park Corner, for example, the older cottages are around the conspicuous pump that was installed as late as 1931, replacing an earlier one.

The most advanced early water supply system in the locality was that incorporated into Hinton Priory. In the Carthusian Order, individual monks lived in their own cottages (the term cell for these gives the wrong impression today), each with a small garden, built around a large quadrangle (see Mount Grace in Yorkshire). Fresh water was supplied to each dwelling by a stone ducted system from springs to the west, and there were drains to take waste away to the east down the valley towards Pond Farm.

In former times the centre of Freshford was often short of spring water, and a stone conduit, a quarter of a mile long, was built to convey water from Sharpstone, along The Tyning, to the church end of the High Street. The high placed hamlet of Pipehouse was also short of water in drought conditions, and a conduit (pipe) was constructed to convey surface water from fields to an enclosed well (house). Thus the possible origin of PIPEHOUSE.

*December 2006*

# 2007

# CHURCH BELLS

It is a longstanding tradition in England to ring church bells at the passing of the old year and beginning of the new. As Tennyson wrote in *In Memoriam* in 1850, 'Ring out the old, ring in the new,…The year is going, let it go'. The diarist Francis Kilvert wrote on this night in 1877: 'I sat up till after midnight to watch the Old Year out and the New Year in. The bells rang at intervals all the evening…and rang on till one o'clock.' Our church towers were built with the express aim of housing bells to mark the times of services, festival occasions, rites of passage, and sometimes times of day such as curfews.

Although the oldest bell in England was cast around 1250, one of the Hinton Charterhouse bells is nearly 550 years old and is thought to have come from Bristol in 1460. Part of the inscription on the bell is *Johannes*, and this might have a link with the dedication of the church to St John the Baptist. The single bell at St Mary's was cast in 1596 and has the initials W.P. of William Purdue a bellfounder from Closworthy near Yeovil. The Cockey family of Frome were famous bellfounders for hundreds of year; Lewis Cockey cast the second Hinton bell in 1687, and William one for Freshford in 1714. With recasting and additions this is now the third bell of the present ring. In recent years the Hinton ring has been made up to three, and Freshford to six. Both new bells came from churches in South Somerset. The Freshford bell was cast in 1911 for Angersleigh, and has an inscription with no intended irony, 'Peace on Earth', an aspiration as appropriate today as it was to Tennyson in 1850: 'Ring out the thousand wars of old, Ring in the thousand years of peace'.

*January 2007*

# COTTAGE LIGHTING

Returning home late on a cold December night, we were confronted by a gang of electricity maintenance men, working to repair our power lines which had broken during the evening. Groping our way into a cold dark house reminded us that electricity is one of the features of modern living that we so easily take for granted. Today we enjoy candles for aesthetic reasons, a surprise to an earlier generation which had struggled to read and sew by the light of candles and lamps, and had sat around the fire hearth, the only warm place in the house:

> And warming-pan, reflecting bright
> The crackling blaze's flickering light.

Until the coming of gas and electricity, candles and oil lamps were essential for domestic life. William Cobbett, born in 1763, wrote: 'I was bred and brought up mostly by rush-light'. Oil lamps were available only from the 1830s, and candles were expensive, so cottage dwellers made their own lights from rushes. The Common Rush is found in most marshy meadows, and was picked during the summer. As Gilbert White wrote in 1775: 'Decayed labourers, women and children make it their business to procure and prepare them.' After being cut and soaked in water for some time, most of the outer green peel is then removed. The rushes are then bleached in the sun, dried and dipped into hot fat, and hung on a piece of bark to dry. A rush of two feet in length would burn for about an hour when held in a rush-light holder. With or without a rush-light, and in the absence of electronic entertainment, a family would often sit around the fire on a winter evening listening....

> Thus dame the winter-night regales

*February 2007*

# DISCOVERIES IN GARDENS

One of the unexpected pleasures of gardening is the discovery of interesting objects in the soil. Particularly common in old cottage gardens are pieces of broken clay pipe. Many of these can be identified as the work of local pipemakers from as far back as the 17th century. Old coins turn up from time to time such as a George II Irish half penny in my own garden.

One of the most interesting finds in this locality was made about thirty years ago in a garden in Park Corner, Freshford. This was a lead disc just over an inch in diameter and was a papal seal, known as a *bulla*, that had some time been attached to a papal document, known as a bull. On one side were the faces of two aged men with SPA and SPE over them indicating St Paul and St Peter. On the reverse side was the name of the specific pope JOHNNES PP II. This is thought to be the seal of Pope John the Twenty-Second, whose pontificate spanned the years 1316-1334 and was based in Avignon in France. It is most likely that the bull was destined for Hinton Priory that had been in existence for around a hundred years. We know nothing of the fate of the books, papers and documents of the Priory after its closure on 31st March 1539. Perhaps they were taken to the edge of their property, i.e. at the edge of their park, Park Corner, and destroyed. In a nearby garden some pieces of medieval tile have also been found that are remarkably similar to remnants at the Priory.

*March 2007*

# VISITING POETS

An interesting person who appeared in the local social round in the 1820s and 30s was the Irish poet Thomas Moore, 1779-1852. He is particularly well known for setting original words to old Irish tunes, such as *The Minstrel Boy* to the *War is Gone* and *The Last Rose of Summer*. He had been living near Devizes since 1817, and was a frequent visitor to the Napier family at Freshford House (Manor). He was particularly complimentary about the Napiers' hospitality, and Mrs Napier's skill in assisting her husband (Colonel, later Sir William Napier) on his six-volume *History of the Peninsula War*.

Another local social centre was Farleigh House, in Farleigh Hungerford, the home of Colonel John Houlton. Here Thomas Moore frequently met another local poet, George Crabbe (1754-1832), famous for his depictions of village and town life, and especially for the poem Peter Grimes, made into an opera by Benjamin Britten. Crabbe was Rector of Trowbridge from 1817 to 1832.

Another regular visitor to the Houltons was Mrs Mary Day (1765-1846) of Hinton House. She kept a diary for many years, much of it concerned with the social round; she evidently met Thomas Moore whom she referred to as Melody Moore, whose songs were frequently sung at the Houltons' social events. She recorded in her diary for July 1827, 'Dined at Colonel Houltons I wore a dove coloured satin dress and gold and ornamental pearl bracelets'.

*April 2007*

# A VISIT OF LELAND

One of the first people to leave a written record of travels around England was the antiquary and poet John Leland. (1503-1552). He had been employed by Henry VIII to give a report on places, buildings, and landscapes. Although this project was not completed, it was published as *Leland's Itinerary* in 1710. In 1542 Leland travelled from Trowbridge to Bath via Farleigh Hungerford, and from here 'rode through woodland for a mile until I came to a large, well-built grange that belonged to Hinton Charterhouse. The priory itself stands not very far away from this grange on the brow of a hill'. It is thought that this grange farm was on the site of the present Hinton House.

He then passed through Hinton towards Midford and saw 'a rough stone wall close to me on my right hand side. Which from its great length looked to have been a park wall. Someone told me later that Hinton Priory originally stood there. About a mile further on I arrived at a village where I crossed by a stone bridge a small brook, which local people call Midford Brook.' From here he travelled on to Bath and Bristol.

In 1545 he was back in this area, and travelled again from Trowbridge to Bath, but this time through Freshford and Lower Stoke. 'After leaving the woodland and the castle and park of Farleigh to my left I rode across Freshford Bridge, which was of two or three new stone arches.' A few years before this the Priors of Hinton and Bath had initiated a collection to rebuild this bridge. (It was rebuilt again in 1782.) From here Leland forded the Wellow Brook near the present viaduct. 'At the very bottom of a steep-sided valley I crossed a wild stream flowing over stones.'

*May 2007*

48

# COTTAGE GARDENS

When a new house is erected today, numerous building, environmental and energy conservation regulations must be adhered to. These stem initially from the Public Health Act of 1875 which for the first time in England laid down regulations regarding house building, such as wall thickness and damp proofing. Yet most new houses today are built with virtually no garden at all. Legal requirements are not concerned about this. This is in stark contrast to an Act of Parliament in 1588 which stated that any cottage newly erected should have four acres of land. This Act was not repealed until the reign of George III in 1775. During this period there were no stipulations regarding the construction or size of a cottage built on a plot.

The end of this legislation corresponds roughly to the time of the more general introduction of the potato into cottage gardens. Previously bread had been the main feature of the cottagers' diet, and their plots of land usually included some wheat for their own bread. Now potatoes were equally important. As a farm labourer's wife from near Calne reported to the Poor Law Commission in the 1840s about her three boys who worked on a local farm: 'they had potatoes and a little tea before they start; they take bread and cheese with them for dinner, and drink water; at night they have potatoes and tea for supper. We have a half an acre of land and get 30 or 40 sacks of potatoes from it'. Many farmers would allow their men an additional plot for potatoes, or as in the case of Hinton Charterhouse in 1834, 20 acres of allotment land for 40 tenants was established on Hinton Abbey land through the efforts of the Rev. Thomas Spencer.

*June 2007*

# UNKNOWN ANCESTORS

The desire to identify our ancestors is as popular today as it has ever been. It is not too difficult to trace family members back to the first part of the 19th century using the National Census returns which commenced in 1801. These are particularly useful from 1841 when the place of birth of each person was recorded. This feature has enabled many to locate places of origin, and to push back the knowledge of family members to the late 18th century. But the generations before this are, to most of us, unknown.

The study of historical records often brings to light individuals, otherwise unrecorded and unremarkable because they are linked to assize or magistrates' records, manorial land tenure agreements, or some other document. In 1243 an assembly of the Somerset Assizes in Ilchester recorded an incident in the life of Felise de Wodewyk. As she was walking along the lane leading to the church of Woodwick, she saw a man lying by the roadside. On closer examination he was found to be dead, but without obvious injury, and was subsequently identified as William le Beo. The Assizes cleared Felise of any suspicion of murder. Who was Felise de Wodewyk? Was she the wife, sister or daughter of Benedict de Wodewyk who, according to the records of Bath Priory of 1232, had a small holding in the parish? We do not know the exact site of Woodwick church which was closed in 1464, although a number of fields near Peipards Farm, Freshford are still called Woodweeks, and one field by the Warminster Road is called Church Powells. We are left with a very brief glimpse into the life of Felise over 760 years ago. But for this she would join the vanished millions who are 'unrecorded, unrenowned'.

*July 2007*

# USEFUL WILD FLOWERS

A relatively short walk around local country lanes in mid-June revealed at least 20 to 30 plants in full flower, as well as numerous grasses. The common names of a number of these give a clue to the long forgotten use and importance of these plants to our forefathers. Hogweed, also known as Cow Parsnip, with large white flower heads, was flowering in abundance. Its hollow succulent stems were gathered by cottagers to feed to their pigs. The attractive small yellow flowered Lady's Bedstraw was used, as its name suggests, spread under a sheet as a soft mattress. It has a gentle hay-like smell when dry, and was also thought to act as a deterrent to fleas. It is known in some areas as Fleawort! The locally abundant Hedge Woundwort with reddish-purple flowers is closely related to the Dead Nettle. It was used to heal wounds by first being bruised, then wrapped around the wound with a cloth. Gerard, in the famous *Herbal* published in 1636, recounts the remarkable healing properties of this plant after 'a poore man in mowing peas did cut his leg with a sithe, wherein hee made a wound to the bones'. Culpeper in the *English Physician* of 1652 wrote, 'It is a very precious herb, and most fitting to be kept in a man's house, both in syrup, conserve, oil, ointment and plaister.'

> Excellent herbs had our fathers of old,
> Excellent herbs to heal their pain,...
> Anything green that grew out of the mould
> Was an excellent herb to our fathers of old.

Rudyard Kipling

*August 2007*

# A CHANGE IN THE CALENDAR

I wonder how we would react if we were told on September 2nd that the next day would be September 14th ? This happened in England in 1752 when the Julian Calendar was changed to the Gregorian, to be in line with most of continental Europe that had adopted this new calendar in 1582. The Julian calendar, introduced in the time of Julius Caesar, had incorrectly calculated the number of leap years, and was now incorrect by 11 days. For many people there was much consternation that they had been deprived of 11 days of their life! This became an election issue and the slogan 'Give us our Eleven Days' was used by William Hogarth on one of his Election series paintings of 1754. Many ordinary village dwellers could not accept the change and, almost fifty years later, the rector of Over Stowey in Somerset wrote in his diary for January 6th 1802 that this was still kept as Christmas Day 'when all the family (of his servant girl, Ann) meet, I find it very much practised among the lower orders in the country'.

At the same time as the calendar change, the first day of the year was changed from Lady Day, March 25th to January 1st. Old copies of the *Book of Common Prayer* state that "the Year of our LORD in the Church of ENGLAND beginneth the Twenty Fifth Day of March'. As a consequence of this change the beginning of the financial year was moved from what was called Old Lady Day to the present day of April 6th. This explains why the Tax Year ends on the unlikely day of April 5th!

*Sept/Oct 2007*

# BENCH MARKS

With the advent of sattelite navigation the Ordnance Survey has no further use for trigonometrical stations commonly known as trig points at the top of many hills and mountains. These are a particular delight to see after a strenuous climb, and many are being restored and preserved by enthusiasts. The more numerous bench marks are also now obsolete. These are horizontal lines carved in stone supported by a carved vertical arrow.

Ordnance Survey surveyors would use these in conjunction with an angle iron, the bench, on which a levelling staff would be supported to calculate the height above mean sea level from Newlyn in Cornwall. Early Ordnance Survey maps from the first half of the 19th century do not show contours or heights above sea level, but have shading to suggest hills and valleys. Large scale maps produced from the middle of the 19th century have contours and bench marks marked B.M. and the height in feet above sea level. More recent maps show the height in metres.

The 19th century surveyors usually carved the marks on long established buildings. With a cursory look around our villages I could find a number of the marks that were shown on maps surveyed in the 1880s, including one on Freshford Bridge (B.M.92.05 feet), the towers of St Peter's and St Mary's, and at Hinton Charterhouse on a wall by the back gate to Yew Cottage in Green Lane. Although a number of the marks appear to have vanished, and their function is now largely forgotten, the term bench mark now has a much wider meaning as a point of reference.

*November 2007*

# WALL PAINTINGS

On a recent trip to South Wales I visited the newly opened St Teilo's Church at the St Fagan's National Museum of Wales. In a unique project that has taken over twenty years, a medieval church from near Llanelli has been moved and rebuilt near Cardiff. It has been decorated and furnished as it might have looked in 1520, just before the Reformation changes. Within and without, the church is lime washed, but additionally the inside glows with colour from a reconstructed rood screen with paintings of the 12 apostles, and repainted wall paintings. These are as identical as possible to those that were painted on the original walls around 1500.

Almost all churches would have been decorated with paintings of saints, such as the popular patron saint of travellers, St Christopher, or of exhortations to upright living. Locally, the most important wall painting is that of St George in St Leonard's Chapel in Farleigh Castle. In the Hungerford Aisle in St Julian's Chuch, Wellow, are representations of Christ and the twelve apostles. Having survived the whitewash of the Reformation, a painting of St Michael vanquishing Satan was destroyed by 'restorers' of St Mary's, Claverton, in 1858. Although no medieval wall paintings have been discovered in St Peter's, Freshford, part of the ten commandments have recently been revealed over the main doorway. These were probably painted in 1766, but whitewashed over about fifty years later.

*December 2007*

# 2008

# FARM NAMES

A recent long train journey from the West Country to the east of Scotland provided an excellent opportunity to observe the variations in farming, buildings and landscape across a four hundred mile transect of Britain. Away from towns and cities, farms with Georgian-style farmhouses indicate the widespread re-ordering of the countryside during the enclosures of the 18th century. Many farms however, have had a continuous existence since medieval times. One that I know on the Wiltshire/Dorset border, was like Barton Farm at Bradford, a grange of Shaftesbury Abbey. On the roof timbers of this house there is a coating of medieval soot from the time when this was a hall-house with a central hearth. Subsequently floors and fireplaces have been added.

The use of the word farm is of relatively recent origin, monastic farms being called granges and others often termed messsuages. The designation 'farm' is derived from a fixed rent on land known as a *firma*. Further back in Anglo-Saxon times an agricultural holding was called a *wick*. The extinct village of Woodwick, located near Peipards farm at Freshford, could be entitled Woodfarm. The name Berwick occurs in Wiltshire, Northumbria and Scotland and means Barley Farm. Wick Farm on the A36 near Brown Shutters is probably the oldest farmhouse in the locality, and has roof timbers dating from 1372. We would no more think of this today as Farm Farm as we would the River Avon as River River!

*January 2008*

56

# CHILD EMPLOYMENT

It is a surprise to realise that schooling in England has only been compulsory since 1880, and then only for children aged five to ten. The school leaving age was raised to 11 in 1893, and by stages to 16 in 1970. Looking at some records of poverty in Somerset in the 18th and early 19th centuries, I was struck by a case of 1822 referring to a 23 year-old man from Radstock who had been working underground as a coal miner from the age of seven. Children, especially boys of this age and younger, were often employed in frightening birds from corn, and they might spend eight to ten hours alone in the fields. This was thought to be the first step in out-door schooling, and was followed by helping their father at hedging and thatching, and then assisting with ploughing and carting.

With the establishment of factories at the end of the 18th century and the expansion of coal mining, the lot of many children deteriorated. A visitor to Hinton Charterhouse in 1827 described meeting children walking from the mills in Freshford. 'I used to fall in with groups of children, down to a very early age, coming from the mills: through the winter they had to be at the mill, two miles off, by six in the morning, not leaving till six in the evening. The children worked the whole day for a very small pittance.'

A few years later in 1833 the Ten Hours Act prohibited the employment of children in textile mills under the age of nine and the maximum of a nine-hour day between the ages of nine and thirteen. A school was opened at Hinton in 1828 largely through the efforts of the vicar, the Rev'd Thomas Spencer. Limpley Stoke School, now the Village Hall was built in 1845, and Freshford School in 1849.

*February 2008*

# COUNTRY WALKING

The recent wet weather has made walking on field footpaths quite difficult. However, not only do we have a variety of footwear for such occasions, we have the alternative of reasonably dry roads to walk or drive on. In the days before motor transport, most village journeys were made on foot, and even roads could be very dusty or muddy according to the weather conditions. As a consequence all churches, chapels, public houses and schools had conspicuous mud scrapers at their gates and doors. There are many good examples of scrapers still in use in our villages. Some appear to have been made by local blacksmiths, while others, such as at the former Methodist church in Freshford, are of ornate cast iron, and are almost identical to those of the Hungerford Arms at Farleigh Hungerford.

Old drawings and photographs show that roadside pavements were a conspicuous feature of our village centre roads many years before the invention of motor transport. Some, such as by The Glen in Rosemary Lane, still show evidence of old paving, and they would have thus provided a clean walkway away from the mud and ruts of the road.

According to a survey in a Berkshire village in 1787, most agricultural labourers had only 'one pair of stout shoes nailed', and their wives 'one pair of strong shoes'. In writing of his childhood in the late 18th century, William Cobbett described the atmosphere of his village church, where 'the parson could not attempt to begin (the service) until the rattling of nailed shoes ceased'.

*March 2008*

# GARDENS AND FARMS

A concern about Food Miles is not something our forefathers would have thought about. Although in medieval times most food would have been grown locally with grain ground in the local mill, yet for the wealthy, spices such as pepper and ginger were imported from India and might have taken up to a year to come via land or sea. Ordinary people such as Griselda in Chaucer's *The Clerk's Tale*, would bring roots, herbs and other grasses to the croft; these she would shred for flavouring. Leeks and herbs would also be grown in their gardens to add flavour to their limited diet. Throughout the centuries gardens have been vital for the survival of village people, and the Second World war slogan 'Dig for Victory' encouraged people to grow as many of their own vegetables as possible. This partial self-sufficiency was also shown in local farming.

In the book *Salute to the Village*, written by Fay Inchfawn (Elizabeth Ward) describing Freshford and Limpley Stoke in the early years of the Second World War, mention is made of six dairy farms in Freshford and Limpley Stoke. Most people would have obtained milk from their nearest dairy farmer, although the amount allowed was actually subject to war-time rationing. Thus cows grazing in the fields had a direct bearing on the life of most individuals in the community. The progressive urbanisation of society and the easy availability of food, albeit now brought from all over the world, has meant that many potentially productive gardens are now used mostly for leisure. Likewise with farm land, many fields are also being taken out of agricultural production for leisure and other usage, and for the first time will not be used for growing crops, or raising animals for meat, milk or wool. Thus the productive toil of the Domesday Book villeins and bordars, and their heirs over thirty generations comes to an end.

*April 2008*

# OLD COTTAGE SITES

There is something rather poignant about seeing flowers growing in an old cottage site knowing that its last occupants are long gone, and all that remains is an overgrown jumble of rubble stones and a few quoins, with a rough outline of a room or two. There are a number of such sites in our villages such as on the track between Dunkirk Mill and Friary, in Ashes Lane in Freshford, and on the rough old trackway that runs from Pipehouse to Midford. It was while walking by this last site in February that I was aware of flowering snowdrops. This cottage was marked on a map of 1824, and it was pulled down in the early 1950s when there was a policy to 'condemn' such properties.

With a bit of good fortune I was able to locate one of the last residents of this cottage. She and her husband moved in in the late 1940s as newly weds. Now aged over 80 and having recently celebrated her Diamond Wedding, she told me of a quiet life here with no gas or electricity, and one tap in a scullery fed from a spring higher up the field. She mentioned the difficulties of bringing coal and pushing a pram up the old trackway, and of her husband going out to collect and saw wood to keep the stove going for cooking. The garden had wonderful soil, and was especially good for growing runner beans. The cottage site near Friary also has drifts of snowdrops and some daffodils. The trees from which Mercy Swift picked fruit and nuts to sell for a few pence are now wild and overgrown, but a few people still remember 'Aunt Merce' and her cottage and garden.

*May 2008*

60

# CLOTH MAKING AND SPINNING

Cloth making in this immediate area is long gone, the last local country mill at Farleigh Hungerford having closed in 1910. Freshford Mill ceased production in 1878, and Limpley Stoke and Dunkirk Mills in 1853. However, manufacture of cloth continued in Bradford, Trowbridge, Frome and Westbury well into the 20th century, finally ceasing at Upper Mill in Trowbridge in 1974. The prosperity of cloth making, especially in the 17th and 18th centuries, is shown by the fine town houses of clothiers. This building legacy is paralleled by an even earlier legacy of trade surnames. In converting sheep's wool into a garment one might encounter the following workers: shepherd, shearer, carder, weaver, fuller or tucker, dyer, clothier, and tailor, all well known family surnames. One that is missing however is spinster. Until the arrival of mechanised spinning in this area in 1790 following the invention of water driven spinning machines by Hargreaves and others in the 1760s, spinning of wool into yarn was by hand. Perhaps in earlier times it was the job of unmarried daughters, hence spinster, but later it was a very common occupation for wives of agricultural labourers. Remembering his childhood in north Wiltshire in the 1780s in the home of an agricultural labourer, Joseph Ricketts wrote: 'I assisted mother and sisters at spinning and carding wool. We had a supply of 20 pounds every fortnight and were paid three pence a pound.' William Cobbett describing the Wylye Valley in the 1770s remembered how 'the women at Steeple Langford used to card and spin dyed wool', while the poet George Crabbe recorded how 'the dull wheel hums doleful through the day'. With the opening of Dunkirk Mill in 1795, specifically for spinning yarn, the hum was gradually heard no more in our village cottages.

*June 2008*

# A VILLAGE BLACKSMITH

The recent discovery in Freshford of an account book of Jacob Holdoway, a blacksmith of Norton St Philip, gives a clear picture of the importance and versatility of this village craftsman. The ledger-shaped book of 224 pages covers a period of 1855-1862, and although much is in very poor condition, it is possible to build up a picture of the range of his work. In this period he had 64 customers, 15 of whom were farmers from as far afield as Tellisford and Shoscombe. One farmer, Mr Cleverley of Hassage Farm, called upon his services 65 times in 1859. This is an exceptional number as the average for farmers was about 30. In addition to hundreds of horseshoes, he repaired threshing machines, ploughs, butter churns, chaff cutters, gates, pumps, cider mills, ground scythes, reaping and hedge hooks, and made rakes, picks and forks. For a plumber and glazier he provided pump buckets, pump rods and nails. He mended a carpenter's vice and provided 'pins' for Mr Holly's water wheel at Norton Mill. For Mr Grist the butcher, he made a new knife and repaired window shutters. For Mr Rossiter a schoolmaster, he repaired a coffee pot and a 'tea kettle,' and for Mr Watts, a maltster, he mended a malt shovel. Among his other customers were a brewer, a mason, a general draper, landlords of the George and Fleur-De-Lys, and the Vicar, Mr Palairet, for whom he provided new bars for church windows, a new lock, repaired a pump, and provided five new hoops for a barrel.

> Week in, week out, from morn till night
> You can hear his bellows blow;
> You can hear him swing his heavy sledge,
> With measured beat and slow.
>
> Longfellow

*July 2008*

# CHURCH MUSIC

The diary of a vicar of a small Oxfordshire town in the 1840s which I am currently reading mentioned that on one Sunday 'there was no singing at morning and evening services, Lymath (the blacksmith) having broken his clarinet'. Until the second half of the 19th century, most village churches relied for music on a small group of singers, usually located in a gallery at the west end of the church, and they used any instruments that were available. We know that Freshford had a singers' gallery, but there is no evidence of instruments until the purchase of an organ in 1868. The Hinton churchwardens' account book, however, reports the purchase of a clarinet in 1815, and new bow for the bass viol (cello) in 1823. Here there might well have been singing in two parts, with the clarinet playing the melody (tune) and the bass viol an underneath part. These instruments were replaced by an organ in 1850, and in turn by the present organ in 1884. St Mary's purchased a harmonium in 1865, and in the 1890s the player was described as the 'harmoniamist' and his train fare was paid to come from Bath each Sunday. The harmonium was replaced by a pipe organ in 1912, and in turn by the present instrument in 1934. The best account of church gallery choirs and instruments is found in Thomas Hardy's *Under the Greenwood Tree*, based on his own village of Stinsford in Dorset. Hardy's characters discuss the relative merits of the different instruments. One claims that 'strings be safe soul-lifters', while another that 'clar'nets be bad at all times, they were not made for the service of the Lard; you can see it by looking at 'em'.

*August 2008*

# TURNPIKES

The recent closure of the viaduct at Monkton Combe for repair work gave an impression of what travel was like in this area before this viaduct and the Warminster Road (A 36) were constructed. The completely new road from Woolverton to Bath was planned by the Black Dog Turnpike Trust in the late 1820s. The Trust had been set up in 1752 and the trustees held their meetings in the Black Dog Inn on the hill between Standerwick and Warminster. One of their earliest toll roads was the Warminster to Bath Turnpike via Norton St Philip and Hinton Charterhouse, now the B3110. Construction of a new road to Bath took place in the 1830s and was planned to be an easier route from the south, by-passing the steep hills at Midford, and that of the Bath Turnpike Trust at Brassknocker.

The viaduct was designed by the Bath City architect George Manners, and was speedily built between January and October 1834. The whole road was opened in 1836. Each turnpike trust publicised its toll charges, and for each section between the turnpike gates fees such as 'For every horse, mule, ass or other beast laden or unladen and not drawing, the Sum of Two-pence. For every drove of oxen, cows or cattle, the sum of Ten pence per Score'. Accompanying the charges there was generally a notice of EXEMPTION FROM TOLLS. These included 'Persons going to or returning from their usual place of religious worship. Horses and carriages conveying the mails. Horses or carriages conveying the arms or baggage of any soldiers or officers. Prisoners sent by legal warrant'. Up to 1854 all turnpikes outside London could charge for a cart pulled by a dog, but in that year an Act of Parliament prohibited their use in this way. A previous Act in 1839 had prohibited their use in London. Thus after 1854 there were no working black dogs on the Black Dog Turnpike!

*September 2008*

# HELPING THE WOOL TRADE

A few years ago there was a campaign to get people to buy British-made goods, the Buy British campaign. More recently households have been encouraged to buy locally produced food and thereby reduce air-miles, and hence carbon dioxide emissions. Both of these campaigns were based on persuasion rather than legislation. In the past Parliament has made laws that would assist the national economy by helping the wool trade. In 1570 an Act was passed which instructed that 'every male over six years old had to wear a woollen cap on Sundays and holy days'. The cap had to be 'made of wool knit, thickened and dressed in England', and the failure to wear one resulted in a fine of three shillings and four pence for each day. This law gave considerable scope for reporting your neighbours, and was repealed in 1597.

Eighty or so years later in 1678 when the wool trade was still in need of support, an Act was passed which ordered that 'no corpse of any person shall be buried in any shirt, shift, sheet or shroud or anything whatsoever other than what is made of sheep's wool only'. Within eight days of burial a member of the family had to submit a sworn statement to the minister of the church (an affidavit) to say that the law had been complied with. Quite heavy fines could be imposed if the law was not obeyed, including fifty shillings given to an informer and a further fifty shillings for the poor of the parish. Many people of substance objected to or ignored this legislation, but were prepared to pay a fine to have their relations buried as they would decide. One such was John Curle, a clothier of Freshford, who died in 1707. In his will he specifically stated that he wished to be 'buried in linen'. This law remained in force for much longer, and was on the statute book until 1814. Perhaps there should be a revival of the woolly hat law to save on central heating costs!

*October 2008*

# OLD TOOLS

It is always pleasing to inherit artefacts which have good associations. I have an old garden spade that belonged to my grandfather, and a four-pronged fork that had been my father's. I like to think of them as I knew them, both digging their gardens or unearthing potatoes with these implements. Such tools were part of the old cottagers' survival kit as growing their own food, especially potatoes, was essential. One of the prizes at the 1865 Freshford and Limpley Stoke Cottagers' Friend Society exhibition was a competition for 'labourers, under 20, who shall dig two perches of ground with the fork in the most efficient manner, and in the most reasonable time'. The first prize was a new steel four-pronged digging fork. For boys under 14 in a similar competition, the first prize was three shillings.

Another implement that I have inherited is an old sickle (reaping hook) marked with the name Fussell. James Fussell had set up an iron foundry at Mells in the middle of the 18th century, and until the final closure of the works in 1894, this firm had been one of the major national suppliers of scythes, sickles, spades, shovels and axes. My sickle must be at least 114 years old, but is still most efficient for cutting long grass. Who knows, but that it might have been used for cutting corn?

From about 1870 the mechanical horse-drawn reaper, and then the reaper and binder were introduced into British agriculture. The reaper and binder is still in occasional use to provide good straight straw for thatching, and during August I saw a magnificent sight of two large fields with rows of stooks from end to end. This was at Marden in the Vale of Pewsey.

*November 2008*

# CHRISTMAS WEATHER

The association of cold, snowy weather with Christmas is remarkably common in Christmas cards and fiction, although in reality it is quite rare in southern England. Charles Dickens' *Christmas Carol*, the story of Ebenezer Scrooge, is told against a background of 'Piercing, searching, biting cold', while Thomas Hardy's Mellstock musicians in *Under the Greenwood Tree* set off to sing early on Christmas morning when 'the moon, in her third quarter, had risen since the snowstorm'. If one looks at diaries and old weather records there evidently have been some exceedingly cold Christmases in the past. In 1796, James Woodforde, the rector of Weston Longville in Norfolk, wrote of Christmas Day: 'the day the coldest we have had yet and frost more severe. It froze all the day long within doors. The cold pieces me thro' almost on going to bed, cannot get to sleep for a long time'.

It is not surprising to find that a chronological survey of agricultural and weather records notes that 'on December 24th 1796 the temperature fell to minus 16°F the lowest temperature on record.' The Rev'd Francis Kilvert wrote of Christmas Day 1879: 'last night is said to have been the coldest night for a 100 years. The windows of the house and church were so thick with frost rime that we could not see out'. Nine years earlier in 1870 he had a Christmas morning experience that we are unlikely to repeat! 'It was an intense frost. I sat down in my bath upon a sheet of thick ice which broke in the middle into large pieces whilst sharp points and jagged edges stuck all around the sides of the tub, not particularly comforting to the naked thighs and loins.' We would no doubt prefer to be with John Clare's shepherd at Christmas as described in *The Shepherd's Calendar* written in 1827.

> Where cottage hearths are blazing high
> And labour resteth from his toils.

*December 2008*

# 2009

# PULPITS

St Mary's Church, Limpley Stoke, is one of only two in Wiltshire to possess a pre-Reformation stone pulpit. The other is Berwick St James. Most pulpits were either hexagonal or octagonal, however that at St Mary's is unusually of only three segments, one for the entrance, and two with two tiers of attractive blank panels. The style is typical of the Perpendicular period between 1450-1500. Because of the unusual structure and placing of the pulpit, it is tempting to think that it might have been obtained from a former monastic building and incorporated after 1578 when the church was described as 'a ruined chapel called Our Lady of Limpley's Chapel', and was being restored back to use. In 1787 a new wooden pulpit was purchased and in the 1870s a visitor wrote 'a heating apparatus was introduced in the form of a common stove placed in the stone pulpit and the pipe carried along the north side, across the gallery and out of the window on the south!'

Many new wooden pulpits were incorporated into churches in the Jacobean period, and two very similar ones are found in the local churches of Westwood (1607) and Tellisford (1608). In the 18th century a large pulpit cushion became an almost standard feature of churches, and in 1770 a Mrs Hill and a Mrs Burchhill were paid £3 for making 'a new cushion and pulpit cloth and tassels' for St Mary's. Freshford pulpit was described in the 1780s as having a 'blue cushion and cloth'. The wit and clergyman, Sydney Smith (1771-1845), described his first Sunday as rector of a remote Yorkshire church: 'When I began to thump the cushion of my pulpit on first coming to Foston, as is my wont when I preach, the accumulated dust of 150 years made such a cloud, that for some minutes I lost sight of my congregation.'

*January 2009*

# WOOD

While recently sawing and splitting some ash logs from a tree in our garden to provide firewood, I thought of a verse from Alexander Pope's (1688-1744) poem *The Quiet Life*.

> Whose herds with milk, whose fields with bread,
> Whose flocks supply him with attire;
> Whose trees in summer yield him shade,
> In winter fire.

Ironically, this tree which I planted 40 years ago, had to come down because it led to the breakage of an electricity wire, and hence the loss of power and heat to a number of houses! Ash wood burns well, but because it is strong and supple has many uses including the handles of garden tools. I am delighted that parts of this tree will be used to make stays for the bells of Freshford church. The stays have an important role in preventing the ringing bell from turning more than one revolution at a time. The use of locally grown timber for tasks was common in former times as most villages had a resident carpenter. A fascinating example of such local use followed the great hurricane in October 1987. In the rural Kentish village of West Peckham, the wooden tiles (shingles) of the spire of the parish church were severely damaged, while in a nearby park some large cedar trees were blown down. These trees were then used to provide the six thousand shingles for the spire.

Until the 19th century and the widespread use of coal for heating and cooking, most people in these parts would have relied upon locally obtained timber. Because there was much wood stealing, certain Acts of Parliament in 1663 and in 1766 attempted to prevent this. The Act of 1766, for example, was for 'the better preservation of timber, trees and of woods and underwoods'. During the 18th century local magistrates had numerous cases brought to them, especially in winter when more fuel was needed for domestic use. In December 1772, James Clark was convicted and fined 40 shillings ' for having in his custody a large bundle of ash wood in the parish of Witham Friary, and not giving a satisfactory account how he came by the same.' Because he could not pay immediately, he was sent to the House of Correction for a month.

*February 2009*

# WIND POWER

Someone travelling today, via Chilcompton and over the top of the Mendip Hills to Wells, would be able to see a recent addition to the landscape near Emborough – a large wind-powered generator. Such electric generators are becoming an increasingly common and necessary feature of the British landscape. Two hundred years ago there were about ten thousand working windmills in Britain, the first having been built around 1200. Part of a tower mill remains on the hillside above Market Street at Bradford on Avon. This seems to have had a very short working life of a few years around 1810. With the advent of steam power, the internal combustion engine and the electric motor, there seemed little use for wind power.

The agricultural engineer John Wallis Titt (JWT) of Warminster wrote in 1897 'in these days of steam and electricity, the power of the wind is not utilized to the extent it might be; under favourable conditions it is more economical than any other'. JWT was the son of a miller from Chitterne, and set up his own business in 1872 to make Wind Engines to pump water. These consisted of a framed tower about 30 feet high with a ring of 40-50 sails. Hundreds of these wind pumps were sold throughout the world, including one for Hinton Charterhouse in 1895. This was installed near Norton Barn, and pumped water to a tank in the centre of the village about a third of a mile away until 1923. JWT's catalogue of 1897 contains a testimonial from the Engineer of the Bath Rural District Council, who installed the pump: 'I have much pleasure in stating that, since the date of the opening ceremony in September 1895, the engine has done its work admirably. During the recent long dry summer a bountiful supply of water was maintained in the store reservoir, and although I took the precaution to have the engine fitted with horse gear in case the wind failed for any length of time, it has not been necessary to spend a shilling for horse pumping. The working cost is but small, there being no expense beyond oiling.'

*March 2009*

# MEDICAL SERVICES

When reading published diaries and letters of the 18th and 19th centuries, one is immediately struck by the crudeness and primitiveness of health and teeth care. Things improved in these villages with the arrival of Dr Thomas Flemming who came to live on The Hill, Freshford, in 1855. In the next one hundred or so years he was followed in the same house by his son Dr Charles Flemming, then by Dr Knox and on the 1st October 1929, by Dr Vaisey. Prior to that time a Dr Adye of Bradford had been employed as the 'parish surgeon' to attend to emergencies, and to carry out inoculations.

In the 18th century blood letting or cupping was a very common practice. An ill patient was supposed to have too much 'morbid humour' and this could be removed by taking blood! Thomas Turner, a Sussex shopkeeper casually wrote in his diary in 1756: 'In the morn Dr Snelling came and ate some breakfast with us and afterwards opened one of the capillary arteries of my temple for the benefit of my eyes. The artery lying deep, the operation was obliged to be performed with a dissecting knife...a second cut hurt me very much.'

The Reverend James Woodforde often had considerable trouble with toothache. Writing in his diary in Norfolk in 1776 he said 'my tooth pained me all night and I sent for one Reeves, a man who draws teeth in this parish, and about seven he came and drew my tooth, but shockingly bad indeed. He broke away a great piece of gum and broke one of the fangs of the tooth, it gave me exquisite pain. Gave the old man that drew it however two shillings and sixpence. He is too old, I think, to draw teeth, can't see very well.' In 1791 he had more success with an interesting form of treatment! 'The sty on my right eye-lid swelled and inflamed very much. As it is commonly said that the eye-lid being rubbed by the tail of a black cat would do it good, and having a black cat; a little before dinner I made trial of it, and very soon after dinner I found my eye-lid much abated of the swelling and almost free of pain.'

*April 2009*

# CHURCH TOWERS

A distinctive and attractive feature of the English countryside is the appearance of church towers and spires marking the distant presence of villages. One of the finest local towers is at St Mary's Church, Westwood. This was built around 1520 with money provided by local clothier Thomas Horton. I have often wondered if it is possible to see the towers of Hinton Charterhouse, Limpley Stoke and Freshford while standing in one public place! I have proved that this is possible while standing at a field gate on Winsley Hill, just before reaching Avon Park. After the richly ornamented tower of Westwood, these three are quite modest, however they still perform the function that they were built for – to house bells. The bells are normally rung before Sunday services, and in the case of St Peter's the clock hours are struck through day and night.

Freshford's tower has an architectural style of post-1450, and we know that money was left in a will of 1514 to assist with the building. This could have taken place over many years as money became available..

The tower of St John's Hinton Charterhouse could date from the late 1100s although the top portion was either rebuilt or added to by the Bath builders, Thomas Jelly and John Palmer. Near the top on the south side one can just read '1770 CW  R  MORGAN' indicating when the work took place, and who was a churchwarden (CW). We know that 15 men were employed to lift the large wooden beams to the top of the tower, and the churchwardens spent three shillings and ten pence in buying beer for them! Near the top of the west side of St Mary's tower carved in a small panel is 'LG  CW  1706'. These are the initials of Lyonell Gibbs who was a churchwarden and shoemaker in the village at that time. These rather modest reminders of past wardens and benefactors contrast with the tower of Stratford Sub Castle near Salisbury, where the tower, rebuilt in 1711, is ostentatiously embellished with huge letters 'THO. PITT  ESQ. BENEFACTOR'.

*May 2009*

# USEFUL PLANTS

It is one thing to read about crafts of the past, but another to try them out in practice.

I have recently tried out two plant-based techniques with modest success! When cottage dwellers could not afford candles, they made their own lights using rushes. In doing this I followed the technique described by Gilbert White in *The Natural History of Selborne* in a letter dated Nov. 1st 1775. I collected some rushes from the River Piddle valley in Dorset, last summer, and by keeping them damp was able to remove most of the outer green peel leaving a long cylinder of pith. This was then soaked in dripping fat and left to dry. A Sussex blacksmith had made a rushlight holder for me, the functional part of which is like a vertical pair of pliers. A rush that I had prepared, which was about a foot long, burnt with a gentle light for about twenty minutes. The light could be described as 'darkness visible,' but it imparted a cosy atmosphere just about sufficient to read by. Gilbert White described how 'little farmers use rushes much in the short days, both morning and evening, in the dairy and in the kitchen.

Recently while clearing our garden of a patch of Jack-in-the-Pulpit or Cuckoopint, and finding some substantial rhizomes, I remembered another name for this plant: Lords and Ladies. This name had been used in Tudor England because the ruffs of the upper classes had been starched using this plant. I thought I would try out this method. Once the rhizomes had been peeled, a white tissue was revealed which I ground in a mortar, adding cold water to produce a thick paste, which was then diluted with hot water. By using a piece of cotton and some embroidered lace (the nearest thing to a ruff), dipped into the solution and dried, the technique succeeded most efficiently! John Gerard, in his famous *Herbal*, first published in 1597, wrote 'the most pure white starch is made of the roots of Cuckowpint; but most hurtfull to the hands of the Launderesse that hath the handling of it, for it choppeth, blistereth, and maketh the hands rough and rugged, and withal smarting.'

*June 2009*

# SCHOOL BUILDINGS

It is quite a common custom to date public buildings, such as schools, chapels and halls, with the year of their erection. When Freshford school was recently enlarged, an end gable was embellished with '2001 Freshford School'. The foundation stone for the oldest building on this site was laid on 23rd September, 1847, and the building 'for the instruction of the children of the labouring poor' was ready for occupation in May 1849. The architect was Francis Niblett of Gloucester who incorporated many delightful decorative features, but no date. In large letters over the inner main doorway is a quotation from Ephesians chapter 5 verses 1 and 2: 'Be ye followers of God as dear children; and walk in love'.

The school at Limpley Stoke (closed in 1932 and now the Village Hall) was opened a few years earlier as shown by the date on the west gable, 1845. Below this are two large gothic letters 'N.S.', the initials of the National Society, or more fully 'The National Society for Promoting the Education of the Poor in the Principles of the Church of England', who gave a major sum of money for the building. Carved over the original main door on to the road in a decorative frieze are words from Proverbs chapter 4, verse 5: Get wisdom, get understanding'.

The first school at Hinton Charterhouse, to which the National Society contributed generously, was opened in Wellow Lane in May 1828. In 1860 a new school (closed in1979) with rooms for both juniors and infants was built near the church to the designs of the architect, William White (1825-1900). Over the doorway of the School are the large letters 'E.J. 1860' of Edward Jones of Hinton House, a major benefactor. Mr Jones subsequently changed his name in 1868 to Edward Foxcroft, and after his death in 1911 was commemorated in a magnificent series of windows in Hinton Church representing influential people in Somerset's history. Appropriately, Hannah More (1745-1833) is commemorated, as she worked hard to establish schools and Friendly Societies in country villages.

*July 2009*

# SAXON CHARTERS

Everyone who owns a house and/or land in this country will have some legal confirmation of this tucked away in a safe or a bank vault. Most documents will have a plan of the precise area of ownership, and this is confirmed by land registry certification.

A thousand years ago, in an era well before maps and plans, major transactions of land were recorded and the 'precise' area described as a clockwise journey around the boundary. There are hundreds of these charters in existence, mostly relating to land given by the monarch to a monastic institution. Because these documents are written in Anglo-Saxon with occasional Latin, they are difficult to decipher. One of 961 granting land in South Stoke by King Edgar to Bath Abbey, includes 'Thonnne on Horscum Wyyllan', which probably means 'Then to springs at Horsecome'.

The most interesting local charter from 1001, is of the estate of Bradford granted by King Ethelred II to Shaftesbury Abbey. The description of this estate, of around one thousand acres, is about the length of this article, and the precise details involve conspicuous features such as rivers, streams, trees, and sometimes the owner of the adjacent land. The description commences at Broughton Gifford, then south-west to the River Bisse, then to Tellisford, and north along the River Frome to Freshford. It then follows the present Limpley Stoke boundary to Midford, back to the River Avon, and then over the high ground to great Chalfield and the stating point at Broughton Gifford. The document commences with 'Arest of seuen pithien on there herewai the schet southward, First from seven pear (or withy) trees on the military road which runs southwards.' Later the charter records that 'it comet to fersefordh thes Abbotes inmare innen Mitford, until you come to Freshford the Abbot's boundary in Midford', i.e. Monkton Combe. Although one cannot find the seven pear trees, many of the other boundary features can still be followed and identified today, over a thousand years later!

*August 2009*

# NORMAN CORBELS

A recent visit to the fine Norman church of St Nicholas at Studland in Dorset showed a wonderful example of the enjoyment that church builders and carvers had about nine hundred years ago. In particular the corbel tables of the nave (corbels are stone projections, usually supporting arches, but used in a line by the Normans to support the eaves of the roof), which were carved as a series of curious faces and animals. In fact the word corbel is supposedly derived from the French word for crow, *corbeau*, as the earliest ones were of birds with very large beaks! Nearer home, the most complete Norman church in this area, at Lullington, also has similar grotesque animals and faces, as well as the most impressive Norman doorway in Somerset. The banishing of these figures to the eaves, might have been symbolic of the banishing of evil to the outside of the building. Later church builders followed this idea, for example, when the tower of St Peter's Freshford, was being built between about 1450 and 1500, a monster on the top of the tower known as an *amphisbaena* with a head and a face in its backside and symbolic of Satan, was therefore left outside. On the other hand, as you went in through the west door (now blocked) and into the church, you would see that this door was guarded by two angelic corbels. The south doorway of St John the Baptist at Hinton Charterhouse is also Norman work, and has two corbels with worn heads of two saints or apostles supporting a moulded arch.

What might be a Norman corbel of ecclesiastical origin, is now at South Cottage, Freshford. For many years it was over an indoor fireplace, then built into an outside wall. It is currently awaiting a new home in an outside wall, where its disapproving presence will be seen again by all!

*September 2009*

# EARTH'S RESOURCES

It is surprising to realize how much use has been made of the earth's natural resources within this area. Most of our buildings are constructed of oolitic limestone obtained from local quarries or mines. Small former quarries can still be seen at Staples Hill and Sharpstone for example, and the Stoke Hill Mine off Midford Lane has been producing large quantities of fine building stone since its reopening in the mid-1980s. The facing stone of the new Southgate development in Bath is from this mine, and there are other mines still working in the Box /Corsham area.

Coal mining came to an end in this area with the last load from Writhlington Colliery near Radstock in September 1973. The Somerset Coalfield had at least eighty colliery sites in the Radstock, Paulton, Timsbury and the appropriately named Coleford areas. The coal seams were narrow and faulty, which made extraction difficult. Thus when the major customer, the electricity generating station at Portishead converted to oil in 1972, the end was near. Mining took place at Foxcote, just beyond Faulkland, until the 1920s. The poet Edward Thomas (1878-1917) on a cycle ride through the west of England in 1917 recorded seeing this mine where 'the white smoke of the collieries drifted slowly in horizontal bands. Carts met us or passed us coming from Rode, Freshford, Frome, to load up with coal from the side of the road'.

Closing just a few years later than the coal mines was the Fuller's Earth works between Combe Hay and Odd Down in 1980. Another works at Tucking Mill between Midford and Monkton Combe had closed in 1940. Fuller's Earth was originally used for degreasing cloth, but subsequently in the pharmaceutical, agrochemical and cosmetic industries, among others.

We certainly do not think of this area in relation to the iron industry, but iron ore was quarried near Westbury Station and in Seend. Blast furnaces operated in both places between 1857 and 1876. Iron ore continued to be mined at Seend until 1946. Lead ore was mined on the Mendip Hills from before Roman times, and was an active industry until the 19th century. Until closure in 1908, there were works for extracting lead from the old slag at Priddy and East Harptree; there was also a silver extraction works at Charterhouse on Mendip in the 19th century!

*October 2009*

# VILLAGE SHOPS

The story of English villages over the last hundred or so years is one of the closure of important service and social facilities such as shops, stations, schools, and chapels. Our local villages have not been immune to this trend as in Freshford, for example, a hundred years ago there were two grocers, one also a baker and post office, a butcher, two other general shops at Park Corner and Sharpstone (also an off-licence), two shoemakers, one tailor, one dressmaker, three public houses, a market garden and a blacksmith/wheelwright. It is therefore a cause of much rejoicing that following the recent closure of the Post Office Stores in both Limpley Stoke and Freshford, leaving once self-sufficient communities with no retail facility, the trend has been reversed with the opening of the magnificent Galleries Shop and Café.

Freshford's retail hub for about 160 years was Morris's Stores in the High Street. This closed as a general store in June 1989, having ceased to be a bakery in 1960, and a Post Office in the 1950s. Throughout its long life it was owned by a continuous family line which passed by marriage from the Watts to the Morris families. Until baking ceased, their horse-drawn and then motorised vans were a familiar site in all surrounding villages. In the 1920s they could be contacted by phone at No 7 Limpley Stoke.

Limpley Stoke's equivalent store from the 1860s was in Middle Stoke near the war memorial. It was often referred to as 'The Wilkins' as this family had owned and run the shop until 1944. Until closure in 1971 this off-licence store was run by the Barnett family. Both of these erstwhile shops had fine display windows and these have been preserved in the conversion to residential accommodation as an appropriate reminder of the past, and perhaps a telling reminder to our generation 'to use or lose'.

*November 2009*

# CHARITABLE GIFTS

An interesting feature of old churches are Benefaction Boards which record for all to see the charitable gift of a benevolent resident. In general they record gifts of sums of money to assist the poor. An unusual gift is recorded at Burford Church in Oxfordshire: Ralph Willet Clerk gave a cow 'for ye benefit of ye poor which was afterwards sold for 10 shillings which sum together with 10 shillings added and is set out to interest for ye benefit of ye poor.' One of the days frequently mentioned for the distribution of an annual gift was St Thomas' Day 21st December, the shortest day of the year and just before Christmas. John Curle of Turleigh and formerly of Freshford, gave land at Chirton in Wiltshire in 1703, the rent of which provided 'Ten shillings to between 30 such poor persons of the Parish of Freshford who have lived by their honest labour.' Just over a hundred years later, in 1817, Thomas Joyce of Freshford House (Manor) left '£100 upon Trust the interest of which to be laid out and distributed in bread on the 4th day every September to such poor who shall not receive parochial relief'. This was two days before the annual Freshford Fair. Both of these charitable gifts are displayed on St Peter's tower gallery.

In Hinton Charterhouse there was a longstanding Christmas tradition, possibly dating back to the time of Mrs Day of Hinton House in the 1820s, and maintained by the Foxcroft family. This was to provide gifts of beef, bread and coal for village residents who worked on the land and had non-earning children at home. The last year of distribution in 1939 was to 27 families, when the gifts amounted to 110 pounds of meat, 39 loaves and over two tons of coal. Miss Helen Foxcroft wrote an account of a distribution that took place about a hundred years ago. The Squire (her father) with a list of names, and assisted by his wife and the chief tenant farmer, would give out meat and bread to each person as their name was called from a table outside the kitchen. Later in the day coal was distributed from horse-drawn carts in the farmyard.

*December 2009*

# 2010

# FONTS

What is the oldest piece of furniture in your house? Most of us have many useful things of the late 20th century, but we often treasure an old family heirloom or antique that we have acquired. Perhaps this is a long case clock two hundred years old, or a piece of Jacobean furniture of the 17th century. When it comes to the age of church furnishings we are in a totally different league. The font at Hinton Charterhouse church is about eight hundred and fifty to nine hundred years-old and is tub-shaped with a typical Norman zigzag design. A few miles south in Lullington there is also a Norman font, and this has a rare Latin inscription: *Hoc Fontis sacro pereunt delictal lavacro* (In this holy font sins perish and are washed away). There are still a number of Saxon fonts in England, one of the most remarkable being at the delightfully named village of Melbury Bubb in Dorset. This is also tub-shaped, but made from a Saxon column with carvings of exotic animals and plants, but all upside down!

During the Commonwealth period in the 1640s and '50s, many fonts were destroyed and replaced by a small bowl, sometimes located within the communion rails. This might have been what happened in both Freshford and Limpley Stoke. We know from the registers that baptisms continued in these churches, although eventually the 'fonts' proved to be inadequate, and new ones were purchased. In 1787 a new font for St Mary's cost one pound, fourteen shillings and fourpence halfpenny. It was carved by a Mr Sumsion, probably a stonemason from Bath. In the same year the churchwardens spent over £12 to purchase a new pulpit and reading desk, and a wooden top for the font. In 1825 the rector of Freshford, George Bythesea, was directed by the Bishop of Bath and Wells to provide a font for his church. The churchwardens 'were ordered to examine the font at Hinton, and to have a font provided for the parish upon the most economical and convenient plan.' They duly purchased one for £4 in 1827 in octagonal decorated style but nothing like the font at Hinton. When the church was described in Arthur Mee's *Somerset* in 1940, he referred to the fact that 'its Norman font is its chief possession'!

*January 2010*

# PROBLEMS FOR TRAVELLERS

The ability to travel easily is something that we take for granted unless it snows, and our local hilly roads and lanes become hazardous. Winter weather, darkness and a lack of maps have always posed a problem for travellers. Thomas Hardy recounts in the Preface to *Under the Greenwood Tree* how village musicians in rural Dorset were handicapped in playing their new Christmas anthem because a pedlar who came every six months with fiddle-strings, rosin and music paper, did not arrive on time. He had been snowed up on the downs, so they had to improvise with whipcord an twine for strings.

When Samuel Pepys and his party were travelling from Salisbury to Bath in June 1668, they got lost on Salisbury Plain and ended up in a remote inn late at night. The landlord turned a pedlar out of bed so Pepys and his wife could sleep there. The next morning he recorded 'up, finding our beds good, but we lousy.' Their journey brought them next day through Beckington and Norton St Philip and on to Bath.

The difficulties of travelling across Salisbury Plain were delightfully described by Richard Barham in his *Ingoldsby Legends* written in 1840:

> No hedges, no ditches, no gates, no stiles,
> Much less a house, or a cottage for miles;
> It's a very sad thing to be caught in the rain
> When night's coming on upon Salisbury Plain.

In the remote village of Berwick St John in the upper Ebble valley between the downs in far south-west Wiltshire, there was an interesting gift to help travellers. The Rev. John Gane, rector here from 1674-1738, left a property in the village the rent of which would pay for the parish clerk to ring a church bell for 15 minutes each evening at 8 o'clock in winter months 'so that travellers in the mist of the hills, could find their way to the village'. This delightful practice was maintained until the 1950s, and the cottage on the site of Gane's original donation is still called Curfew Cottage.

*February, 2010*

# OLD TECHNOLOGY

Modern technology has become so complex and sophisticated that we hardly wonder any more at the invention of the next i-something or other. However, one can imagine the amazement in 1922 when in this rural community, and with crystal set permitting, a voice from London could be heard! From January 1927 'wireless' broadcast was by the BBC who subsequently in November 1936 commenced television transmission.

According to the historian Diarmaid MacCulloch, the most complicated machines that a medieval person would encounter in their life would be the pipe organ, the clock and the (wind) mill. Although all three of these machines are easily replaced by something electronically hi-tech, they can all still work with medieval technology and natural power. Although the churches of Hinton Charterhouse, Freshford and Limpley Stoke have pipe organs built in the second half of the 19th century, and with 20th century electric blowers, it is still possible to power all three by hand pumping. (Most useful in power cuts.) One still has the satisfaction of hearing the sound generated by the passage of wind across the lip of a pipe as in the Pan-pipes first recorded in 250 BC.

The tower clock in St Peter's Freshford was installed in 1860 and replaced another of unknown age. It is a fine example of a posted cage clock and is still powered by weights hand-raised about 30 feet twice a week. The strike weight is about three hundredweight (around 150 kg.) and the clock weight about half that size. The technology is basically similar to the working clock in Salisbury Cathedral that was constructed in 1386.

There has been a tremendous revival of stone flour milling with wind or water power in the last few decades. Few mills have had continuous production by these means throughout the 20th century, an exception being Cann Mills near Shaftesbury. The harnessing of water power, albeit for electricity generation, is an exciting local prospect. Mills for flour production were recorded in all three of our villages in 1086 (*Domesday Book*), and the earliest in England was from around 762.

*March 2010*

# PARLIAMENTARY REPRESENTATION

O n a recent trip to Salisbury we took the road from the north that passes quite close to the spectacular ramparts of the former cathedral city of Old Sarum. From the time of the foundation of the new Salisbury Cathedral and city in the valley below in 1220, Old Sarum went into decline. The political agitator and reformer William Cobbett (1763-1835) rode by Old Sarum on horseback in August 1826 gathering information on the state of agriculture and the poor, to be published later as *Rural Rides*.

He continually referred to Old Sarum as the 'accuresed hill'. Old Sarum was a classic case of a Rotten Borough which had lost its population, but still had two Members of Parliament. Until the Parliamentary Reform Act of 1832 which gave a more uniform representation, Old Sarum, with only 13 electors, could nominate two MPs as could a town like Dunwich in Suffolk which had mostly fallen into the sea. Developing new industrial cities such Manchester with a population of over 133,000 had no specific representation. This was changed by the much debated and hard fought for Reform Act, but even then few people could vote unless they had property of a particular value.

I have a copy of a Somerset Electoral Register for 1832, and Freshford with a population of over six hundred had 21 electors, six of whom were non-resident. Hinton Charterhouse also with a population of over six hundred had 32 electors, five of whom were non-resident. Smaller parishes such as Tellisford had five, and Hardington only two. It was to be another hundred years after the Reform Act of 1832 and the culmination of many Acts of Parliament, that the Representation of the People Act in 1928 eventually gave the vote to all men and women over 21. In 1969 this was reduced to the age of 18. With election fever in the air, it is interesting to think of the agitation, campaigning and demonstration that was needed over one hundred and fifty years to give us all the right to vote for an MP. William Cobbett would be delighted with the outcome, but perhaps not with some MPs!

*April 2010*

# OLD MALTINGS

In our local community we are familiar with the presence of old industrial buildings that have been converted for use as offices or houses. Of especial historic importance are those that were involved with cloth production: Limpley Stoke Mill, Freshford Mill and Dunkirk Mill. Some other industrial buildings that remain were associated with malting and brewing. At Clearbrook Farm at Midford a large malting has recently been converted into living accommodation. Attached to the brewery at Freshford there was also a large malting which, after ceasing to be used over a hundred years ago was used, among other things, as an architect's office, and now as living accommodation. A modern malting is now high-tech and scientifically controlled, and a far cry from these 19th century country maltings with their own spring water.

In the early 19th century Warminster was the West of England malting capital. In 1818 there were over 25 maltsters, and these would have provided malted barley for numerous breweries in Wessex. Miraculously, one of the old Warminster maltings in Pound Street has been preserved, and malt is still produced in the very traditional way that it would have been at Clearbrook and Freshford in the 19th century. There is no shortage of demand for this product as it is sent to breweries as far afield as Greenland and New Zealand. The building has thick walls and long low floors, and with shuttered openings, a relatively uniform temperature is maintained.

Barley grain is first treated for three days in a cycle of 12 hours water and 12 hours rest, and then as it begins to germinate it is spread on the floor about five inches deep. The grain is still turned by an ancient hand plough three times a day. After about five days of germination, the grain is heated in a kiln to reduce the moisture content, and then, after the shoots have been removed, bagged for use. In the brewing process yeasts will convert the malt sugars from barley grain starch into alcohol. The old English word for barley was *bere*, and a barn a *beren*, a barley-room.

*May 2010*

88

# NATURAL DISASTERS

The recent disruption of flying caused by an Icelandic volcano might have been unprecedented, but the influence of volcanic ash has certainly been noticed in England in the past. The Rev'd Gilbert White (1720-1793), whose natural observations of his village in Hampshire as a series of letters were published as *The Natural History of Selborne* in1789, wrote graphically about such an event in June and July of 1783, although he was unaware of its cause. In his Letter LXV to Daines Barrington he wrote

> 'the peculiar haze, or smokey fog, that prevailed for many weeks in this island and in every part of Europe, was a most extraordinary appearance, unlike anything known within the memory of man. The sun, at noon, looked as black as a clouded moon, and shed a rust-coloured ferruginous light on the ground, and was particularly lurid and blood coloured at rising and setting. The country people began to look with a superstitious awe at the red louring aspect of the sun; and indeed there was reason for the most enlightened person to be apprehensive.'

From his parsonage in Norfolk, James Woodforde wrote in his diary for June 25th 1783 'very uncommon lazy weather. The sun very red at setting.' We now know that the cause of these effects was the eruption of an Icelandic volcano called Skapter-jokull. Perhaps the greatest eruption in recent history was of Krakatoa between Java and Sumatra in August 1883 which was heard three thousand miles away, and caused a tsunami drowning 35,000 people. At least three months after this occurrence, there were still spectacular dawns and dusks in England. In the following year occurred the most severe earthquake to be recorded in England. The so-called Colchester Earthquake in 1884 damaged around twelve hundred buildings, including twenty churches. The tower of St Nicholas' Church at Little Wigborough was entirely demolished.

*June 2010*

# CLEARING WOODLAND

Having with considerable effort recently grubbed up a number of smallish seedling trees using heavy metal tools such as a pickaxe and saws, I can really appreciate the magnitude of the task that our forefathers had in felling and clearing trees and bushes to create cultivatable land. As much of our cultivated land has been in continuous use for hundreds, if not thousands of years, and was certainly cleared in the era of hand tools, it makes one realize that almost every square metre of land that so easily vanishes under concrete (or now in town gardens, under paving or gravel), was brought into use by an immense amount of human endeavour. The landscape historian Oliver Rackham describes this as 'the greatest achievement of any of our ancestors'. In most manorial settlements after the Norman Conquest, the clearing of woodland was regulated so that each community had adequate arable, meadow and pasture, but also sufficient woodland for fuel, building materials, fencing and implements and tools. Many of our local woodlands are a legacy of this legislation. If land is not cultivated or hedges are not cut, woodland or woodland belts are reformed. Old cottage sites at Friary and near Midford, untouched for fifty or more years, are now like small copses.

Also requiring considerable effort in past times was the conversion of grassland to arable for crop growing. Even removing a small lawn is quite a labour. This must have happened to a large field on the Freshford-Limpley Stoke border at Pipards Farm that is called Burnbake(s). Well over two hundred years ago, when the name was first recorded, turves were pared off, put into piles and burnt. In this way the soil would have the nutritional gain of the plant ash. Although this name remains, the field is now grassland again, unlike 'The Pastures' at Westwood, which is anything but pasture!

*July 2010*

# OLD NEWSPAPERS

Some people save newspaper cuttings or even whole newspapers, for such times as the day World War Two ended or the Coronation of Queen Elizabeth II. What is fascinating is to find old newspapers in unexpected places. About forty years ago we purchased a small wooden trunk from a departing Freshford resident. The bottom of this was lined with a *Bath and Wilts Chronicle and Herald* for 10th June 1947. It had eight pages and cost a penny and a half. This paper provided a brief snapshot of life here 63 years ago. The one advert on the front page was for Camp Coffee and Chicory Essence. The L.M.S. Railway Co. 'Require males aged 16 to 24 years to train as locomotive firemen'. There is a report on the first concert of the newly formed City of Bath Bach Choir.

An even more unexpected find are old newspapers that were used to line wooden partition walls, and were overlaid with wallpaper. In the former Post Office in Freshford, one side of a wall was covered with *Pictorial World* from 1876 and 1879. In the former was part of an illustration of a ceremony connected with the Star of India in Calcutta. On the reverse side of the wooden partition was part of a Bath newspaper with typical late Victorian adverts for Macassar Oil, and Clarke's Buffalo Biscuits for dogs. The Queen's Huntsman declared 'I have decided to use your biscuits in the Royal Kennels.' Also Weaver and Son of Broad Street, Bath, were advertising products from their Steam Power Bedding Manufactory. An even more extensive find was from a wall in The Old Parsonage at Freshford. These newspapers date from 1859, the year a new Rectory was built. There are examples of *The Bath Express* for June 18th 1859, the *Weekly Mail* sent to 'Mrs Fisher, Freshford, Somerset' with a Victoria penny stamp. There are also a number of pages from the *Kentish Gazette*, dated Canterbury, 8th November, 1859.

*August 2010*

# TUNNELS

One of the most unusual developments taking place locally is the restoration of the Combe Down railway tunnel. It was constructed in the early 1870s for the railway line linking Bath with Wellow and then on to Radstock and eventually Bournemouth. The last train (steam) ran on this, the Somerset and Dorset line, in March 1966. The tunnel is over a mile in length (1,829 yards), and is being restored as a cycle path and walkway linking Bath with Midford.

Perhaps one of the most famous railway tunnels in England is the nearby Box Tunnel that was completed in 1841. At almost two miles long (3,212 yards), it was then the longest tunnel in Great Britain. The whole project was described as being 'monstrous, dangerous and impracticable', and in the early years ladies were taken over the top by carriage as passage though the tunnel was supposed to be constitutionally damaging! Building of the tunnel was certainly damaging, as over a hundred navvies died in its construction. The line from Bristol to London via Bath and Box had originally been given approval in 1835.

This led, in this era of 'railway mania', to numerous other ambitious railway schemes. One of these was for a branch from the Great Western Line in Bath to Warminster and Weymouth. Joining the main line near Bath Station, the branch would have passed by a mile and a half long tunnel from Widcombe to Monkton Combe. Then along the Avon valley to Limpley Stoke where one line would continue to Warminster, while the Weymouth branch entered a tunnel that passed under the Crowe Lane-Freshford Lane corner, cutting across The Tyning near the present school, to run up the River Frome valley. One can imagine how different the centre of Freshford would have been if this scheme had not been abandoned and a line from Bath built up the Avon valley to Bradford and beyond.

A tunnel that was built much earlier and still survives in excellent condition, but on private land, is a 135 yard long tunnel in Wellow under the road just east of the church. This was built around 1804 for the Radstock branch of the Somerset Coal Canal. This arm of the canal was never completed, and the canal was replaced by a narrow rail trackway on the towpath. This conveyed coal to Midford until it was sold to the emerging Somerset and Dorset Railway in 1871.

*September 2010*

# HEARTH AND WINDOW TAX

The state of our nation's economy is at present never far from the news headlines. Throughout history governments have sought new but fair ways to tap the wealth of individuals to support the state and its functions. One of the more unusual forms of taxation was enacted soon after the Restoration of the Monarchy in 1662 – the hearth tax. This was the major source of government revenue until it was abolished in 1689. The tax was levied twice a year, on Lady Day and Michaelmas, at the rate of one shilling per hearth. From the outset it was unpopular as Samuel Pepys noted on June 20th, 1669: 'They clamour against the Chimney-money and say they will not pay it without force.' The collection was made by officers known as 'Chimney Men', who collected money from each house, and could take goods if the tax was not paid within one hour. Those who violently resisted could be imprisoned for one month. The 'Chimney-Men' were allowed to search each house once a year to find 'what Fire Hearths or Stoves are increased or decreased'. Exemptions were made for those too poor to pay parish rates or whose property was less than £10 in value.

Some of the lists of hearth tax payers have been published, and from Freshford in 1664 we know that there were 20 households ranging from one with 11 hearths to two with one. There were a few exemptions for payment such as for two houses being rebuilt, in other cases one chimney had been pulled down and another had fallen down. Two were excused 'by reason of their poverty'. Knole House in Sevenoaks, sometimes described as the largest private house in England, paid for 85 hearths!

The hearth tax was abolished in the early years of the reign of William and Mary in order to gain popularity. However government revenue needed to be raised, and a window tax was introduced in 1697. Each householder paid at the rate of two shillings each year with an additional payment of eight shillings for a house with over 10 windows. This tax was abolished in 1851.

*October 2010*

# CHAPELS

Church towers are such an identifiable and familiar feature of English parish churches, that it is easy to pass by less conspicuous non-conformist chapels. In the 17th century they were often made from a converted cottage or made to look like one with domestically proportioned windows and doors. Following the Toleration Act of 1689 Protestant non-conformists were allowed to worship in premises that were licensed. Within these three parishes we have five erstwhile chapels that have become houses!

The earliest is part of the Methodist Church at Sharpstone, and was built in 1782. John Wesley, the founder of Methodism, visited Freshford eight times between 1750 and 1782. His followers had formerly met in a cottage in Sharpstone, but he wrote in his diary after his last visit he opened the new house at Freshford. At that time it was known as Shaston Meeting House. In the 1860s a new chapel was built next to the old one which then became the schoolroom, and was a place of worship until 1995. In 1814 a small Methodist chapel was built inconspicuously behind number 20 High Street, Hinton Charterhouse. This chapel closed in 1965. For some, the original Wesleyan Methodism was not radical enough, and a number of breakaway groups emerged. One of these was the Primitive Methodists who were closely allied to agricultural trade unionism. In 1873 they built their own chapel in Freshford at the intersection of Rosemary and Abbey Lanes. Village locals referred to this chapel as the prims. With the coming together of the various Methodist groups in 1932, this chapel closed in 1937.

There has been a long tradition of Baptist non-conformity in Southwick, near Trowbridge, since the mid-17th century. Arising from this early foundation were numerous chapels in West Wiltshire, including the one at Limpley Stoke. Following informal meetings from 1811, the Baptist Chapel in Middle Stoke was opened on January 1st, 1816. During the 19th century adult baptisms were carried out in the River Avon. This chapel had a major rebuild in 1888, but closed down in 1984. A Mission Hall, called the Village Room, was opened by this chapel at Pipehouse in 1903, but closed in 1974.

*November 2010*

94

# CHRISTMAS WAITS

Carol singing around our villages is the continuation of a long tradition that goes back into the mists of time. In the 18th and early 19th centuries, carols were sung by the church choir members (this was the time when unrobed men sang from a gallery at the west end of the church), with an accompaniment of a few instruments, if available. The best description of such a group of singers is found in Thomas Hardy's *Under the Greenwood Tree*. It was the practice in the village of Mellstock, a thinly disguised description of Stinsford in Dorset, to sing only after midnight on Christmas Eve, as just before the clock struck twelve they lighted the lanterns and started. Hardy describes the four men and seven boy singers with a cello and three violins. Singing in the early hours of Christmas morning around the parish was not appreciated by all, especially Farmer Shiner, who roared from his window , 'Shut up, don't make your blaring row here!' The stoical minstrels nevertheless carried on. These men would have fitted the description of Christmas minstrels by William Wordsworth, written in 1819:

> Keen was the air, but could not freeze,
> Nor check the music of the strings;
> So stout and hardy were the band
> That scraped the chords with strenuous hand!

There are a number of descriptions of actual singers recorded in diaries and journals. The Rev'd James Woodforde described how on Christmas Eve at Ansford in Somerset in 1764, 'the singers came very late this evening, and they sang a Christmas Carol and an Anthem and they had cider as usual'. Across to the north-west of the county at Overstowey in 1799, the Rev'd William Holland noted carol singing was very early on Christmas morning: 'I sent half a crown to our Church musicians who had serenaded the family this cold morning at five o'clock.' At Christmas two years later, he wrote, 'the singers at the window tuned forth a most dismal ditty, half drunk too and with the most wretched voices'.

The poet John Clare for December in *The Shepherd's Calendar* published in 1827, gives a vivid picture of a rural cottage Christmas. Carol singers also appear on Christmas morning, and attempted to achieve an impossibly high standard of singing!

> The singing waits, a merry throng,
> At early morn, with simple skill,
> Yet imitate the angels' song,
> And chant their Christmas ditty still.

*December 2010*